Cambridge Elements

Elements in Data Rights and Wrongs
edited by
Megan Richardson
University of Melbourne
Rachelle Bosua
Deakin University
Damian Clifford
Australian National University
Jake Goldenfein
University of Melbourne
Jeannie Marie Paterson
University of Melbourne
Julian Thomas
RMIT University

DATA RIGHTS IN TRANSITION

Rachelle Bosua
Deakin University

Damian Clifford
Australian National University

Jing Qian
University of Melbourne

Megan Richardson
University of Melbourne

Shaftesbury Road, Cambridge CB2 8EA, United Kingdom

One Liberty Plaza, 20th Floor, New York, NY 10006, USA

477 Williamstown Road, Port Melbourne, VIC 3207, Australia

314–321, 3rd Floor, Plot 3, Splendor Forum, Jasola District Centre, New Delhi – 110025, India

103 Penang Road, #05–06/07, Visioncrest Commercial, Singapore 238467

Cambridge University Press is part of Cambridge University Press & Assessment, a department of the University of Cambridge.

We share the University's mission to contribute to society through the pursuit of education, learning and research at the highest international levels of excellence.

www.cambridge.org
Information on this title: www.cambridge.org/9781009613514

DOI: 10.1017/9781009613545

© Rachelle Bosua, Damian Clifford, Jing Qian, and Megan Richardson 2025

This publication is in copyright. Subject to statutory exception and to the provisions of relevant collective licensing agreements, no reproduction of any part may take place without the written permission of Cambridge University Press & Assessment.

When citing this work, please include a reference to the DOI 10.1017/9781009613545

First published 2025

A catalogue record for this publication is available from the British Library

ISBN 978-1-009-61351-4 Hardback
ISBN 978-1-009-61355-2 Paperback
ISSN 2976-7520 (online)
ISSN 2976-7512 (print)

Cambridge University Press & Assessment has no responsibility for the persistence or accuracy of URLs for external or third-party internet websites referred to in this publication and does not guarantee that any content on such websites is, or will remain, accurate or appropriate.

For EU product safety concerns, contact us at Calle de José Abascal, 56, 1°, 28003 Madrid, Spain, or email eugpsr@cambridge.org

Data Rights in Transition

Elements in Data Rights and Wrongs

DOI: 10.1017/9781009613545
First published online: August 2025

Rachelle Bosua
Deakin University

Damian Clifford
Australian National University

Jing Qian
University of Melbourne

Megan Richardson
University of Melbourne

Author for correspondence: Rachelle Bosua, r.bosua@deakin.edu.au

Abstract: *Data Rights in Transition* maps the development of data rights that formed and reformed in response to the socio-technical transformations of the post-war twentieth century. The authors situate these rights, with their early pragmatic emphasis on fair information processing, as different from and less symbolically powerful than utopian human rights of older centuries. They argue that if an essential role of human rights is 'to capture the world's imagination', the next generation of data rights needs to come closer to realising that vision – even while maintaining a pragmatic focus on effectiveness. After a brief introduction, the sections that follow focus on socio-technical transformations, emergence of the right to data protection, and new and emerging rights such as the right to be forgotten and the right not to be subject to automated decision-making, along with new mechanisms of governance and enforcement.

Keywords: data rights, privacy, socio-technical transformations, fair information processing, pragmatism

© Rachelle Bosua, Damian Clifford, Jing Qian, and Megan Richardson 2025

ISBNs: 9781009613514 (HB), 9781009613552 (PB), 9781009613545 (OC)
ISSNs: 2976-7520 (online), 2976-7512 (print)

Contents

	Introduction	1
1	Megan Richardson, Precursors and Threads	2
2	Rachelle Bosua, Rise of the Computer and Catalysts for Change	12
3	Jing Qian and Megan Richardson, From Pragmatism to Activism	23
4	Damian Clifford, Making and Remaking Data Protection	33
	Conclusion	45
	References	48

Introduction

In this Element we map the development of data rights that formed and re-formed in response to the socio-technical transformations of the post-war twentieth century.[1] Like other human rights movements, the modern data rights movement – once it was established as being about *human* rights, that is, about the 'dignity and worth of the human person', as stated in the Preamble to the Universal Declaration of Human Rights (UN General Assembly, 1948) – can be characterised as an effort to frame an ideal society underpinned by a liberal-dignitarian ideology. However, modern data rights themselves also seem quite pragmatic, in keeping with the minimalist visions of their post-war architects.[2] Thus, they are rather different types of rights from the utopian human rights of older centuries, which were fashioned grandly to frame a new world order in the wake of revolutions and subsequently formed the principal subject matter of the Universal Declaration. Not surprisingly, they have attracted their share of deep criticism. We argue that if an essential role of human rights in today's (and tomorrow's) world is 'to capture the world's imagination', as Samuel Moyn (2010: 47–48) puts it, the next generation of data rights needs to come closer to realising that vision, even while maintaining a pragmatic focus on effectiveness and enforcement.

This is not to say that the essential idea of data rights as human rights needs to alter fundamentally. As spelt out in the Preamble to the United Nations' International Covenant on Civil and Political Rights in 1966, elaborating on the Universal Declaration, human rights are based on 'the inherent dignity ... of all members of the human family', as the foundation of 'freedom, justice and peace in the world' (UN General Assembly, 1966, Preamble). We would say that is as true of our rights over the data that defines, constitutes, and concerns ourselves as of our other rights to enjoy 'civil and political freedom', per the Preamble to the International Covenant. However, we argue that these rights are best viewed not as fixed in time and place but as constantly evolving under the impetus of the experiences and imaginations of their authors and subjects, in the same way as at their inception.[3] Viewed this way, data rights represent a mode of

---

[1] Of course, these were not the only important socio-technical transformations that prompted social concerns and shaped ideas about rights, for example, to privacy: consider earlier photography, telephone, phonograph, cinema, wireless telegraphy, radio, and television (Warren & Brandeis, 1890; Beniger, 1986; Lake, 2016; Richardson, 2017).

[2] Note that the nomenclature of data rights geared to data processing may vary. For instance, in Europe the label 'data protection' is commonly deployed as distinct from 'privacy'/'private life', while in the US (and Australia) the language of 'privacy' is generally used across the board, or 'data privacy' may be a surrogate for data protection (and cf. Bygrave, 2014: xxv). In this Element we tend to follow the European delineating approach.

[3] Thus, we see data rights as a reflection of both social activism for rights and more pragmatic deliberation about how to frame and give them effect (cf. Dembour, 2010, on 'protest' and 'deliberative' schools of human rights).

'responsive law', responding to ideas of 'civil morality' (Nonet & Selznick, 2001: 16). The need for human rights to respond to ideas of civil morality is recognised in the Preamble to the Universal Declaration, when it states that 'the advent of a world in which human beings shall enjoy freedom of speech and belief and freedom from fear and want has been proclaimed as the highest aspiration of the common people'. Unfortunately, we do not see quite the same ethos of responsiveness when it comes to proclaiming data rights beyond the traditional rights to privacy, family, home, and correspondence in Article 12 of the Universal Declaration and Article 17 of the International Covenant. Rather, the development of data rights has largely been a feature of heterogeneous efforts in post-war years. We argue that, while there have been significant achievements, more is needed if we are to approach an imaginary of a data society shaped by a shared social ethic of human rights – what Danielle Celermajer and Alexandre Lefebvre (2020) refer to as human rights as a 'way of life' (22).

In the following sections of this Element, we focus on key stages in the development of data rights from the 1950s to the present day, opting for a periodisation that reflects also our own individual and collective experiences. We finish with a slightly hopeful speculation on the data rights movement's future frontiers, including the rise of new and emerging data rights and governance and enforcement regimes. As such, we offer a kind of panoramic view, finding this useful even while appreciating that it can never fully represent 'the multifarious practices of everyday life' (Nelson, 1997: 40).

1 Megan Richardson, Precursors and Threads

1.1 Three Themes

In the 1950s, the decade in which I was born, data rights underwent profound changes. At the beginning of the decade, the Universal Declaration of Human Rights (UN General Assembly, 1948) and European Convention on Human Rights (Council of Europe, 1950) had just been agreed, and the UNESCO human rights exhibition was beginning its world tour (see Charlesworth, 2021). But already shattering any myth that these widely popularised rights texts would automatically result in more protection of human rights, George Orwell (1949) in England had also just produced *Nineteen Eighty-Four*, where he pointed out how in the post-war era people could still quite easily become subjugated to totalitarian systems of technologised surveillance, file-keeping, and bureaucratic doublespeak. And Hannah Arendt (1949) argued in the *Modern Review* that millions of displaced people still failed to enjoy 'the right to have rights' given the state-centric terms of the Universal Declaration (and, it might be added, also the European Convention prior to the rise of the European Court of Human Rights with jurisdiction to hear individual claims; see Bates, 2010).

Even apart from these obvious problems, as I have argued elsewhere (see Richardson, 2023a), a difficulty from the beginning was the list of rights in the Universal Declaration and European Convention. Both drew heavily on traditional human rights such as the right to privacy/private life as provided for in Article 12 of the Universal Declaration and Article 8 of the European Convention.[4] Privacy at that time was still seen largely in terms of an intimate sphere of 'privacy, love and friendship' (Orwell, 1949: 30): a private sphere for the sharing of 'confidences and intimacies' (Cowen, 1969: 10). In the language of the official French version of the Universal Declaration, it was a right to '*[la] vie privée*'. Or as elaborated by Samuel Warren and Louis Brandeis in 1890, it was a right to 'the privacy of private life' (Warren & Brandeis, 1890: 215), encapsulated in their formulation of this as (a species of) 'right to be let alone' (Warren & Brandeis, 1890: 195) – an article drawn on closely in Associate Justice Brandeis's critique of untrammelled electronic surveillance of citizens by the state in his leading dissenting judgment in *Olmstead v. United States* (1928). And there was no apparent right geared to modern systems of data processing. That came later in Europe, with support found in the rights to dignity and free development of personality in Articles 1 and 2 of the German Basic Law (Federal Republic of Germany, 1949), a modern rights text compared to the Universal Declaration and European Convention. But still in the 1950s, even after the insidious data processing and dehumanising racial profiling of the Second World War (see Kempner, 1946), there was no felt need for a right to data protection that might protect data subjects directly. It was as if privacy and data processing went in separate streams: the first finding support in the post-war human rights texts, the second thought of as lying outside the domain of rights.

Instead, the principal domain of data processing in this period was the economic domain. The work of German sociologist, lawyer, and political economist Max Weber enjoyed a revival in post-war America, with his posthumous 1921 masterwork *Law and Economy* (*Grundriß der verstehenden Soziologie*), including its arguments for efficient bureaucracy as the most effective form of modern government, becoming the subject of close study and analysis at the University of Chicago (see, for instance, Shils & Rheinstein, 1954). The field of law and economics, also based at the University of Chicago, was just taking off, and it

---

[4] Such rights have a long tradition, including in law, being acknowledged in judicial statements and legislative pronouncements in diverse jurisdictions dating back over centuries (even if they featured less commonly in constitutions, per Diggelman & Cleis, 2014); see Richardson (2017).

represented a major shift away from the ideas of those like Associate Justice Brandeis who criticised 'the curse of bigness' in business (Brandeis, 1934). The Chicago lawyer-economists' arguments for efficient markets operating effectively where business operations were allowed to flourish free of government intervention were exemplified by Ronald Coase, who in 'The Federal Communication Commission' (Coase, 1959) and 'The Problem of Social Cost' (Coase, 1960) took further his reasoning in 'The Nature of the Firm' (Coase, 1937) of the efficiency of firms in minimising transaction costs, to argue that firms could efficiently navigate social benefits and costs. Less attention was paid to how the efficient power of firms could produce human costs, for instance, for data subjects who as a result of their technologies and systems could become easily identified and tracked by authoritarian governments, as (it was later argued) occurred in Germany during the 1930s and 1940s (see, for example, Black, 2001; McCormick & Spee, 2008).

At the same time, and again quite separately from the human rights discourse, there was a growing fascination with human-machine relations. In 'Computing Machinery and Intelligence', published in *Mind* in 1950, pioneering British computer scientist and wartime code cracker Alan Turing posed the question, 'can machines think?'. Turing concluded that there were indeed 'possibilities of [this occurring in] the near future, rather than [just being a] Utopian dream' (Turing, 1950: 442). In the United States, likewise, science writers were imagining future human–machine relations in largely utopian terms (the more dystopian accounts would come later). For instance, Isaac Asimov provided a hugely popular fictional vision in his *I, Robot* short story series, published in various science fiction magazines from the 1940s and in book form in 1950 (Asimov, 1950), with its robots of the twenty-first century contributing to the benevolent rule of the intergalactic system, operating by 'Three Laws of Robotics' (per the *Handbook of Robotics*, 56th edition, 2058 AD) built into their 'positronic brains',[5] namely:

1. A robot may not injure a human being, or, through inaction, allow a human being to come to harm.
2. A robot must obey the orders given it by human beings except where such orders would conflict with the First Law.
3. A robot must protect its own existence as long as such protection does not conflict with the First or Second Laws.

Although Asimov wrote mainly about robots, he also wrote about intelligent computers. In 'The Last Question', published in *Science Fiction Quarterly* in

---

[5] For a current take on these laws as a baseline for regulating artificial intelligence, see Pasquale (2020).

1956, he explores the idea of a very intelligent computer's response to a question raised by generations of humans of how to address the heat death of the universe. The answer, 'INSUFFICIENT DATA FOR MEANINGFUL ANSWER', is repeatedly given until the last intelligent computer, AC ('AC' standing for 'automatic computer' in 'ancient English'), correlates and puts together in all possible relations all the data collected over 100 billion years to conclude that entropy is possible. Note that human beings and their data are not ultimately the central focus of this futuristic story. Indeed, both become increasingly indistinct as the story progresses, and '[o]ne by one Man fused with AC, each physical body losing its mental identity in a manner that was somehow not a loss but a gain' (Asimov, 1956: 14). As the godlike AC declares at the end of the story, 'LET THERE BE LIGHT!!', adding, 'And there was light' (Asimov, 1956: 15).

So how, then, did an embryonic idea of data rights begin to emerge out of these disparate threads by the end of the decade, with the process of change continuing in subsequent decades?

1.2 Transformations

Still at the end of the 1950s and indeed up until about the mid 1960s, the right to privacy/private life was conceived primarily as a right to private and domestic life, data processing was conceived primarily in economic terms, and computers were primarily seen as enhancing rather than threatening human life. But the seeds of change were already there. While later in this Element we argue that in subsequent decades popular sentiment against ubiquitous computerised data processing systems deployed by governments and large business enterprises (often in tandem) helped to generate a shift towards a new conception of data rights, we see some precursors in the immediate post-war decades.

Firstly, consider the impact of changes taking place in the contours of private life. In 1890, Warren and Brandeis (1890) were already talking about how socio-technical changes involving the 'too enterprising press, the photographer, or the possessor of any other modern device for recording or reproducing scenes or sounds' (206) were impacting on 'the sacred precincts of private and domestic life' (195). Their particular impetus for writing the article may have been unwanted press reporting of the Warren family 'weddings, social gatherings and funerals' (Gajda, 2008: 42). But already, writing at the *fin de siècle*, they could offer a more modern example of violation of privacy as being the 'somewhat notorious' case of surreptitious photography of actor Marion Manola's performance while dressed in tights in a Broadway theatre (Warren & Brandeis, 1890: 196, citing *Marion Manola v. Stevens & Myers* (1890)). By the post-war 1950s, the traditional idea of a private life centred on domestic activities and walled-off private spaces was coming under threat from multiple sides. And, even if it was not completely lost, the distinction between private and public life was more attenuated. In part this was due to technological changes, but in part also to the way that people lived their lives. With cameras by now both commonplace and inconspicuous, photography easily captured intimate moments in transient semi-public places, from fairgrounds to marketplaces to wedding venues (see, for example, *Lea v. Justice of the Peace, Ltd* (1947); *Gill v. Curtis Publishing Co* (1952); *Gill v. Hearst Publishing Co.* (1953); cf. *Victoria Park Racing v. Taylor* (1937), between the wars, discussed in Richardson, 2023a, 2023b). Building design further added to this opening up of previously 'private' areas with large windows and limited walls (see Colomina, 1994), with the office a particular example of a 'private' place being made easily accessible with the use of current technologies.[6] As detailed neatly by Donald King and Marwin Batt (1961: 18),

> [d]uring the last few years, a number of instruments which can be used for surveillance have been developed. Within this new era may be found tiny transmitters placed in the pen on the desk, in the telephone receiver or in the eagle emblem on the wall; special microphones to pick up conversation from the opposite side of the wall or 'through open windows hundreds of yards away ... '. Other instruments for visual surveillance are also being perfected.

Government surveillance of citizens' lives was a notable feature of these Cold War years, making use of these technological and architectural affordances. Offices, meeting rooms, and hotel venues, along with private homes and public streets, became targets for secret surveillance of 'left-of-centre' political figures such as Martin Luther King and Mohammed Ali in America (see Pilkington, 2013) and communist party members, trade union leaders, and peace activists in Britain (see Ewing et al., 2020). In Australia, Herbert Vere Evatt, leader of the Australian Labor Party and former president of the United Nations General Assembly (when it approved the Universal Declaration of Human Rights, in 1948), was caught up in the surveillance operations of the Australian Security Intelligence Organisation (ASIO), established by the Labor Chifley government in 1949 at the behest of the US and UK (see Manne, 1987; Cain, 1990: 3–4). Those within Evatt's political orbit were subjects of ASIO surveillance, along with leaders of the post-war peace movement, union executives, civil servants,

---

[6] *Olmstead v. United States* (1928) offers an intermediate example of surveillance of business and family life within a mixed home–office environment, with Brandeis J (dissenting) arguing that the right to privacy should be drawn on to address government agents' secret telephone tap under a broad reading of the US constitutional right against search and seizure provided in the Fourteenth Amendment. This became the Court's position by the 1960s, in a case of surveillance of a public payphone: *Katz v. United States* (1967).

and members of the left-wing migrant Soviet community (see Cain, 1990; Nilsson, 2023). Some turned out to be Soviet spies, most famously Vladimir and Evdokia Petrov, whose ASIO-instigated defection prompted a Royal Commission, while others lived out their lives under a panopticon-like existence of ubiquitous real and imagined surveillance (Nilsson, 2023: 585). Evatt, who appeared at the Royal Commission in support of his staffers made subject to ASIO surveillance (see Figure 1 below), objected to ASIO's alleged political allegiance to the Liberal Party, led by Robert Menzies, and undermining of the Labor Party, which had lost the election in May 1954 in the wake of the Petrov Affair.

Evatt was eventually barred from the commission and some judged him already to be suffering from the mental health issues which plagued him in later life, his mind 'unbalanced' by the Petrov Affair, as Menzies put it (Manne, 1987: 263). But by then ASIO's name was 'severely blackened' in the eyes of the labour movement, which also largely accepted that ASIO had 'colluded' with the prime minister to stage Petrov's defection, to win the election (Cain, 1990: 8–9).

Figure 1 Dr Evatt appears at the Royal Commission on Espionage, 16 August 1954. Ern McQuillan, public domain image reproduced courtesy Mitchell Library, State Library New South Wales.

Secondly, clearly it was not just about acts of surveillance. That data obtained through surveillance could be stored in files, transmitted, shared, and potentially used even in unexpected ways against data subjects was evident in light of scandals like the Petrov Affair in Australia. And while much file-keeping was relegated still to paper files and punch cards in the 1950s, by the 1960s computerisation increased this exponentially. By the second half of the 1960s, public concerns in Europe about risks associated with computerised data processing would provide the impetus for early data protection regimes – beginning with the Data Protection Act of 1970 (Hesse, 1970), followed by the Swedish Data Act (*Datalagen*) of 1973 (Sweden, 1973) and the West German Federal Data Protection Act (*Bundesdatenschutzgesetz*) of 1977[7] (Federal Republic of Germany, 1977) – and, while the first was limited to the public sector, the second and third extended more broadly to the private sector as well (see Hondius, 1975: 34–38; 44; González Fuster, 2014: ch. 3).

Even before these European initiatives, a catalyst for law reform in the US was the publication of journalist Vance Packard's *The Naked Society* (1964), which revealed that already in that country '[t]here are banks of giant memory machines that conceivably could recall in a few seconds every pertinent action – including failures, embarrassments or possibly incriminating acts – from the lifetime of each citizen' (Packard, 1964: 29–30). Packard's exposé was directed as much at business as at government.[8] But his most stringent critique was reserved for the US government (the major client of the mainframe computer), including his Orwellian vision that '[i]f information is power, Americans should be uneasy about the amount of information the federal government is starting to file on its citizens in its blinking memory banks', adding that '[o]bviously these memory banks are useful tools ... But what are their implications for two decades from now, in 1984?' (Packard, 1964: 42). In June 1965, the US House of Representatives launched a public inquiry into 'invasion of privacy', followed by a second session on 24 May 1966 focused on computers (United States House of Representatives Special Subcommittee, 1965; 1966). Around this time, also, came the publication of political scientist and lawyer Professor

---

[7] The Swedish Data Act (*Datalagen*) of 11 May 1973 was the first national law on data protection in Europe (see Hondius, 1975: 44).

[8] Not all activists (in the 1960s and even the 1970s) were as intent as Packard on arguing for data rights covering business. Consider, for instance, well-known consumer activist Ralph Nader, who was made the target of a surveillance and file-keeping operation conducted on behalf of General Motors (with the company secretly engaging former FBI agent Vincent Gillan to carry out the operation) after publication of Nader's (1965) stringent critique of the company's safety practices, in *Unsafe at any Speed*. Nader's case for breach of privacy was settled with a substantial payout: see *Nader v. General Motors Corporation* (1970). Nevertheless, he did not treat this success as a reason to extend his social activism to questions of data rights of data subjects, being focused rather on '[a] well informed citizenry ... [as] the lifeblood of democracy' (see Nader, 1970: 1).

Alan Westin's studies of data processing practices, including *Privacy and Freedom* (Westin, 1967), and *Databanks in a Free Society* with Michael Baker (Westin & Baker, 1972). In the words of Michel Atten (2013), it was Westin who especially 'brought the biggest underlying questions into the public arena', enabling arguments for citizens' data rights to move beyond the press, the academy, and the government elites – even if (like Packard earlier) he had to stretch the traditional language of 'privacy' to encompass these modern concerns, namely, as extending to the collection, use, storage, and so forth of personal information (Westin, 1967: 7). For instance, the Advisory Committee on Automated Personal Data Systems of the US Department of Health, Education & Welfare (1973), chaired by RAND engineer Willis Howard Ware, drew on Westin's work in its 1973 report on *Records, Computers and the Rights of Citizens*. As discussed in Sections 2.2 and 3.2 of this Element, the above studies and reviews helped shape the US Privacy Act of 1974 (United States Congress, 1974).

Thirdly, increasing computerisation made automated decision-making a potential feature of (rather than a phenomenon distinct from) data processing. Already in 1964, Richard E. Bellman of RAND Corporation, speaking at a conference on cybernetics and automation in New York, observed that the combined effect of technical affordance, considerations of efficiency, and pressures of competition would mean that automation (namely 'the ability to carry out operations of decision making and technology with either no human supervision or else greatly reduced manpower requirements') would inevitably come to dominate industrial production and decision-making processes (Bellman, 1964).[9] A few years before, Bernard S. Benson, of the Benson-Lehner Corporation, speaking on the social implications of information processing in a radio talk hosted by UNESCO in Paris in 1959, foreshadowed the need to consider the risks (as well as the potential benefits) associated with 'automatic machines which are able to remember' for the human subjects of data processing, pointing especially to risks such as the perpetuation of 'falseness', 'misconceptions', and 'misunderstandings' about targeted individuals. And, at least by the second half of the 1960s, there were more general public

---

[9] 'Cybernetics' refers to a term coined by mathematician Norbert Wiener (1948) to explain what he saw as the central features of the new scientific field of computer science, namely scientific modes of communication and control. By 'control', Wiener meant logical decision-making, rather than, per 'sensationalist' journalism, mindless totalitarian 'control of human beings by automata' (see Hilton, 1966: xi–xii). See, likewise, Wiener (1950) and Bellman (1964) (both more concerned with pointing to the human benefits to be gained with freedom from the drudgery of mindless repetitive work, which could now be handed over to machines). Although Wiener at least gestured to the risk of letting a machine 'decide our conduct, unless we have previously examined the laws of its action, and know fully that its conduct will be carried out on principles acceptable to us!' (Wiener, 1950: 212).

fears (superseding the initial enthusiastic reception) of the 'risk of abuse', especially on the part of the post-war generation which was now 'coming of age', about the effects of 'technocracy' (Hondius, 1975: 7).

The US Privacy Act was content to treat 'automated' data processing alongside other types of data processing carried out by federal government. But in Germany automated data processing was a focus of the Federal Data Protection Act (*Bundesdatenschutzgesetz*) (Riccardi, 1983: 250), although this Act in general applied to other types of processing as well (Hondius, 1975, 37). As to France, the Law on Information Technology, Data Files and Individual Liberties (*Loi relative à l'informatique, aux fichiers et aux libertés*), of 1978, drew a distinction between automated and non-automated data processing, applying more stringent standards of consent and legality to the former (González Fuster, 2014: 64–65). This law also stated, in section 2, that no legal, administrative, or private decision involving an assessment of human conduct should be based (in the case of a legal decision) or solely based (in the case of an administrative or private decision) on the automated processing of information that provided the profile or personality of the person concerned (*traitement automatisé d'informations donnant une définition du profil ou de la personnalité de l'intéressé*). Such provisions may be seen as responding pragmatically to what Bygrave describes as the 'real danger' of '[automated] profiling operations resulting in unfair or unwarranted assessments of data subjects' (Bygrave, 2002: 310). However, as Gloria González Fuster (2014: 63–64) explains, an inspiration for the French drafters was a broader commitment to the value of liberty. Consistent with this was the statement in section 1 that information technology must be in the service of the citizen (*l'informatique doit être au service de chaque citoyen*), noting also the importance of human identity, 'the rights of man', private life, and individual or public liberties (*libertés individuelles ou publiques*).

Nevertheless, despite the embryonic language of 'individual or public liberties' in the French data protection law of 1978, it would be hard to conclude that there was widespread acceptance of the idea of data rights as civil rights and human rights on the part of lawmakers by the 1970s. The West German Constitutional Court (*Bundesverfassungsgerich*) may have recognised 'the free will of the individual' as protectable from state encroachment (Pharmacy Case, 1958: 668), but it was yet to unite this idea with a right to informational self-determination, as came later in the Census Act Case of 1983 (and helped to inspire the right to data protection in the EU Charter of Fundamental Rights (European Union, 2000, 2007: Article 8), as discussed later in this Element. The US Privacy Act of 1974 may have referred to 'the right to privacy' as 'a personal and fundamental right protected by the Constitution of the United States', and concluded that 'in order to protect the privacy of individuals in information systems maintained by Federal agencies, it is necessary and proper for the Congress to regulate the collection, maintenance, use, and dissemination of information by such agencies' (United States Congress, 1974: section 2). But, as Packard points out (1964: 323–324), this right – at least when he was writing in the mid 1960s – was not (in the US) understood as extending against business and other private organisations. We might expect it also to extend beyond the simple catalogue of 'fair information practice' principles regarding the collection, maintenance, use, and dissemination of data to encompass a more expansive array of data rights geared to the preservation of human liberty in the face of increasingly technologised data processing. As to Australia, its Privacy Act came only in 1988 (Commonwealth of Australia, 1988), and although it may have referred to 'the right to privacy' in the Preamble, this was hardly viewed as a significant feature of the Act, which provided for *de minimis* data protection standards (at that stage only for government agencies, and exempting practices of intelligence agencies) following the broad contours of the principles approved by the Organisation for Economic Cooperation and Development (OECD) in 1980. And, when 'the right to privacy' was referred to in the Preamble, the reference point was strictly the right to privacy in the International Covenant of 1966, which did little more than restate the right in the Universal Declaration of 1948. Even so, in all these disparate threads, with their insistence on the current importance of privacy and data protection, we see a precursor of sorts for what later was to emerge as a larger movement for rights-based law.

1.3 Foreshadowing the Emergence of Data Rights

In conclusion, the changes taking place in the 1950s and early to mid 1960s described in this section produced some useful reforms in the framing of early data protection/data privacy standards in the 1970s. They did not represent a fully fledged data rights movement. But the seeds were there in, for instance, Packard's *The Naked Society*, and in public responses to scandals like the Petrov Affair that exposed surveillance for public view, as well as in occasional statements from maverick insiders like Benson, in his UNESCO radio talk. They offered an important foreshadowing of what was to come. As noted in later sections of this Element, the data rights movement of the 1970s and 1980s would involve bigger buy-in from activists. Moreover, it would garner significant support from a wider array of individuals and groups, along with other 'stakeholders', including from those who found themselves subject to widespread surveillance and other forms of data processing. Thus, we start to see that, if rights emerge through a struggle, as Rudolph von Jhering argued in the nineteenth century (and I have come to think myself),[10] they gain potency when it is as a struggle in which all society participates.

2 Rachelle Bosua, Rise of the Computer and Catalysts for Change

2.1 A New Computer Science Industry

Prior to considering the impact of the rise of computing on the emergence of data rights, it is worth briefly describing early developments of computing devices. Many of these took place in the three or four decades following the 1950s, the main period of this section. Based on considerable advances in engineering, computational devices evolved from the early 1930s to the 1950s into large stand-alone computing devices in the 1960s. The focus was on computing and engineering techniques to advance all aspects of computing, moving away from simple desk calculators to larger, more complex machines. A series of successful commercial electronic computers, called 'mainframe computers', was developed that flourished in the processing of data in the 1960s and 1970s. Examples of applications were largely in the business and military domains, including ballistic missile systems in submarines, satellite navigation systems, and business systems, such as IBM's first development of the airline reservation system SABRE in 1964. The development of mainframe computers with the ability to integrate distributed data paved the way for further advances in developing minicomputers with hardware architectures extending to communication networks in the mid to late 1960s. In the mid 1970s, microcomputers followed, based on rapid advancements in computer technology, in particular the design of the microprocessor,[11] which sparked and facilitated early design and extensive development efforts to refine microcomputers into the personal computers that we have come to know today.

A result of these developments was that computing power and the processing of business and individuals' data (collecting, storage, access, manipulation, and reuse of personal data) were brought closer to those who manage and use the data, namely, database managers, smaller entities, and ultimately individual users of personal computers. Developments in channels for computer networking and communications technologies in the mid 1970s further facilitated communication and collaboration between users and business entities.

---

[10] See von Jhering (1879: 1–2). I explore this idea further in Richardson (2015).

[11] A microprocessor component embeds data processing logic and control on a single integrated circuit (IC) or multiple ICs. The component contains the arithmetic logic and control circuitry needed to perform the functions of a computer's central processing unit.

However, as I argue below, it was only with experience of the internet, invented in the early 1980s and rapidly escalated in its use in the 1990s and beyond, that those in the industry came (over time) to view their activities through a more socio-technical lens. In the early days, the predominant focus within the industry was largely efficiency and efficacy. And for those who thought more deeply, and more idealistically, the prevailing ethos was one of freedom from control – little realising that what were ultimately being controlled were data subjects.

Notably, major computing and programming developments in this period were predominantly led by the US, with some interest and influence coming from other parts of the world, such as the UK, Japan, and Russia (O'Regan, 2021), as well as France (Mounier-Kuhn & Pégny, 2016) and West Germany (Donig, 2010). Likewise, as detailed in Section 1, these were the centres of political contestation around what should or should not be done with these radical new technologies – with the Europeans leading here in terms of early data protection regimes, followed shortly (and in a more limited way) by the US with its Privacy Act of 1974. My interest in this section is particularly what those in the nascent computer industry thought about these developments and initiatives. Those located in outposts like South Africa, the Netherlands, and Australia, where I studied and worked, did not participate in the debates. Indeed, like most of my fellow students starting out their undergraduate degrees in computer science at the University of Pretoria in the 1970s, I was unaware that the era was labelled the 'Information Age' in far-off America (ASIS, 1978). Rather, our focus was essentially technical. We started our coursework with unravelling the combination of mathematics, mathematical statistics, and computer science as a basis to better understand the machine and in particular learning *how to program the machine*. In the course of our study we investigated and applied a variety of scientific and business-oriented programming languages (i.e., Assembler, Lisp, Common Business-Oriented Language (COBOL), and later Programming Language 1, (PL/1)) to better understand how the 'machine' manipulates different types of data. The highlight of my programming education was the writing of computer applications in COBOL, capturing data and process instructions that were processed on a large computer using IBM's 12-row x 80-column punch cards. Leaving the university, I then started my analyst/programming career programming in PL/1.[12] As a young

---

[12] PL/1 is an imperative, procedural computer programming language with an English-like syntax to describe complex data formats with a wide array of functions to verify and manipulate the data. PL/1 was initially designed and developed by IBM for scientific, engineering, business, and system programming. PL/1 and later versions thereof was used continuously by academic and commercial institutions from the 1960s into the 1990s.

programming professional, the notion of data rights in my computer science education was unknown territory. The language of data protection was coming into use by this stage, but it was viewed more from a computer security perspective than a dignitarian perspective in software engineering and computer security circles. While there were early signs of a data rights movement in the 1960s and 1970s, with some forward-thinking computer scientists participating in debates about data rights, it was only in the 2000s and beyond (with experience of the internet) that computer scientists *as a larger group* started to embrace the nascent data rights movement.

2.2 Early Focus on Transparency and Information Security

Notwithstanding the wide-ranging concerns about 'privacy' voiced by journalists, civil society groups, and some individuals in the 1960s and 1970s, as foreshadowed above, the predominant focus in industry circles in this period was ultimately on increasing the level of transparency and control around data processing practices (consistent with information security) without undermining the practices entirely. Inevitably, I would say, this bureaucratic mindset had some influence on the shape of data protection/data privacy standards in this period – especially in the United States and only to a somewhat lesser extent in Europe. This is clear from the 1973 report on *Records, Computers and the Rights of Citizens*, from the US Department of Health, Education & Welfare Advisory Committee on Automated Personal Data Systems (1973: xx–xxi), chaired by RAND engineer Willis Howard Ware, which inspired the 'fair information practice' principles of the US Privacy Act of 1974 (United States Congress, 1974). It states as follows (US Department of Health, Education & Welfare, 1973: 41, italics omitted):

> Safeguards for personal privacy based on our concept of mutuality in record-keeping would require adherence by record-keeping organisations to certain fundamental principles of fair information practice.

- There must be no personal-data record-keeping systems whose very existence is secret.
- There must be a way for an individual to find out what information about him is in a record and how it is used.
- There must be a way for an individual to prevent information about him obtained for one purpose from being used or made available for other purposes without his consent.
- There must be a way for an individual to correct or amend a record of identifiable information about him.

- Any organisation creating, maintaining, using, or disseminating records of identifiable personal data must assure the reliability of the data for their intended use and must take reasonable precautions to prevent misuse of the data.

As can be seen from the above quotation, while there were some 'privacy' concerns from those in the computer science industry, given its role of advising government about the processing of data in the 1960s and 1970s, these concerns were predominantly to do with the security of data once collected, and the storage of data. From an industry perspective, data storage was an essential component of any data processing system. In contrast to wider social concerns about the effects of practices around data processing (i.e., the collection, storage, extraction, and commercialisation of data processing involving citizens and organisations for citizen data rights), the government perspective was quite different, being more closely aligned to the perspective of industry professionals (cf. O'Mara, 2018, who also notes this influence). For instance, despite public protests about data processing voiced by American citizens, journalists (such as Vance Packard, author of *The Naked Society* (Packard, 1964)), civil rights groups, and student activists under surveillance by the FBI and lawmakers; and despite reports issued by the congressional special subcommittee in 1965 and 1966 calling for greater 'privacy' controls, as detailed in Section 1.2, on the government and industry side it was clear that there were perceived benefits in using computers to engage in data processing without strict legal limitations. And, even when some regulatory standards began to emerge in the US, in the form of the Privacy Act of 1974, the aim was not to restrict the large bureaucratic databases used by the US government to store personal information but rather to set 'reasonable' parameters (e.g., Westin, 1967; Westin & Baker, 1972). In terms of establishing and maintaining standards, much was still left to the professional standards and practices of those manning computers and their advocates.

As to business uses, there was little need seen for legal regulation on the part of industry insiders – a position that at least initially was embraced by governments as well, especially in the US.[13] This perspective is not surprising in an efficiency-driven economy which places a high value on innovation. After all, computing evolved exponentially in terms of size, power, speed, and capability in the 1960s and 1970s. From the 1960s, the focus was on the collection and processing of business data through large, centralised mainframe computers, treating data mainly as a key entity that adds business value. In the 1970s,

---

[13] As to European jurisdictions such as Germany and France, coverage was more mixed (see Section 1).

database systems became more sophisticated through the use of database management systems (DBMS)[14] that used underlying data models to structure and manage data. This allowed for the separation of data from program instructions whereby records, files, and data sources could be converted into machine-exploitable electronic data. This new realm took automation to the next level and opened up new avenues for mechanisation in data processing labelled as: automated data processing, integrated data processing, or electronic data processing in big corporations (Haigh, 2001). Business transactions focused on the processing of customer and vendor data into meaningful information that could impact and guide business transactions. In the business world, the focus was therefore mostly on the collection and storage of business data using centralised databases and the further processing of this data into information using dedicated business-oriented programming languages. In addition, computing and early system development focused on attaining business value through financial business transactions and the development of standards allowing for the exchange of information (processed data) between different computers and different computer manufacturers. In all this, the human perspective on data protection/data privacy, in particular the collection and processing of personal data (e.g., customer data), was not being given serious consideration in industry circles at this time. But even beyond that, 'solutions' to problems of 'privacy' that were essentially understood in terms of information security were seen as largely solvable at the organisation and industry level, without the need for specific legal standards to be imposed from the government side.

2.3 The 'CIA Triad' of Information Security

In short, while the need for information security standards was accepted by Ware and other insiders as extending even to their own systems and practices, their focus in coming up with 'solutions' was largely internal rather than external (at least outside of the public sector, where some regulation was supported). Not that they did not see the need for 'solutions' to what was clearly a growing problem from the 1970s onwards. With the increase in cybercrime in the 1970s (and even before that; see Chadd, 2020), computer security emerged as an important discipline in the training and work of computer science professionals. The Advanced Research Projects Agency Network (ARPANET) research project, in 1972, catalysed the cybersecurity era. ARPANET was a precursor to the internet that was formally introduced in 1983. This project

---

[14] A DBMS software application allows users to create, define, manipulate, and manage a database through ways to organise, store, and retrieve large amounts of data in an organised, quick, and efficient way. DBMSs enforce data integrity (accuracy, completeness, and quality of data), ensuring that data is secure, and facilitate the management and analysis of data.

identified challenging vulnerabilities in emerging networking technologies and automation, with multiple US organisations collaborating to develop automated techniques to detect vulnerabilities in software. In the same way as currently, the computer security disciplines of the 1970s and 1980s focused on the *reliability* of rare and high-priced computing machines, with information protection mainly achieved by controls of physical access to computers (Cherdantseva & Hilton, 2013). As computer hardware and software became more affordable, protection changed from computers processing raw data into information to the protection of data/information itself. Information security (InfoSec) was born and defined as practices to protect information by mitigating information risks (Whitman & Mattord, 2021). Its central idea was that specific controls were required to prevent unauthorised or inappropriate access to data, the tampering thereof, or any activities that might impact the integrity of information, thereby protecting data from a security perspective.

In short, information security risks resting on the three pillars of the confidentiality, integrity, and availability of information (commonly referred to as the CIA triad) were identified, with measures to mitigate information risks associated with each (see Bell & La Padula, 1976; Clark & Wilson, 1987; Spafford, 1988).[15] The nascent InfoSec discipline also provided guidelines on how threats to an organisation's data and information assets could be identified and mitigated through appropriate risk analysis methods, along with insights into the value of design. And it argued that an organisation should design and manage its information architecture, applications, and systems with each of the CIA principles in mind (Whitman & Mattord, 2021) through the design, development, and implementation of its own policies and self-regulatory mechanisms to protect its data against any imaginable threat. By doing so, organisations may cover every possible way of protecting their sensitive data from ever-increasing cybersecurity threats and attacks. A number of International Organization for Standardization (ISO) and National Institute of Standards and Technology (NIST) standards were developed to support organisations in the development of their own InfoSec risk management frameworks. These standards still play an important role in maintaining information security in the industry.[16]

---

[15] In computing circles, the idea of availability of information gained prominence in 1988, when the first version of a computer worm (probably the first internet worm) emerged, created by Robert Morris, from MIT.

[16] Both NIST and ISO are leading standards bodies in cybersecurity that are still used today. NIST SP 800-53 is a US government security standard that provides a comprehensive set of security and privacy controls for federal information systems. ISO 27001 is an international standard that provides a framework for an information security management system to protect an organisation's information assets.

Why, then, did fears about information security not prompt arguments for new legal standards geared to strengthening information security across the board in this period? One reason was the computer industry's early confidence it could handle the risks associated with security issues. Moreover, even where threats were seen as particularly serious, especially where government data processing was involved, there were already some protections available through early US data protection/data privacy standards (see, for example, Ware, 1979). Indeed, when one looks closely at the 'fair information practice' principles framed by Ware and his colleagues on the US Department of Health, Education & Welfare (1973) Advisory Committee on Automated Personal Data Systems, with its focus on protective mechanisms and access controls, we can see how information security was a principal concern.[17] Likewise, in Europe in the 1970s, where the concerns were more broadly to do with data protection/data privacy and regulation was not necessarily restricted to the public sector (as in the US), there was still a focus on bureaucratic 'fair information practice' principles in many of the early laws, as noted in Section 1.2 (and see also Hondius, 1975: 6).

Rather, the most significant step in thinking about data rights occurred after the birth of the internet in the early 1980s, as discussed in Section 2.4. It was only with that step, which moved computer processing into radically new fields, that a significant number of computer scientists, with input from behavioural and social scientists, came to see information security as something that could not just be managed internally, and data rights more broadly as rights that the law should strive to protect.

2.4 The Birth of the Internet, 1983 Onwards

Since its inception, the internet has been one of the most significant computing developments to challenge data protection/data privacy and data rights more generally. The formal adoption of Robert Khan and Vinton Cerf's ARPANET communications model (at the time labelled the 'modern internet'), in January 1983, standardised data transmission in multiple networks (Hauben, 2007). Many scientists and engineers had collaborated to realise their vision of an internet long before the technology to create this was ready or invented. For example, in the 1900s the inventor Nikola Tesla had the idea of a 'world wireless system', and in 1960 computer scientist Joseph Licklider published

---

[17] Ware himself, reflecting back on the work of the US Department of Health, Education, and Welfare Advisory Committee in the 1980s, suggests that its code of fair information practices was geared more generally to good 'record-keeping' and if there was any historical analogy for the practices it was to be found not in privacy but in fair labour practices updated to take into account the need for 'computer security' challenges of modern data banks (see Ware, 1980: 12-15).

a paper that articulated the idea of networked computers that provided advanced information storage and retrieval of information (Licklider, 1960) – following this up in 1968 with a paper, with Robert Taylor, that anticipated the computer as a communicating device operating across multiple networks (LickLider & Taylor, 1968). An important practical step from the computer science and engineering field came in 1965 with the development of 'packet switching'.[18] This method of transmitting electronic data, which became a building block of the internet, enabled the first message delivery between a computer located at the University of California in Los Angeles and another in Stanford using the ARPANET network, with the first four-computer networks up and running in December 1969. From this point onwards computer networking in the form of private networks emerged, and networking and communications technology advanced rapidly in the 1970s up to the birth of the internet.[19]

The 1990s became undoubtedly the 'epoch of the internet', first as a result of new networking and communication architectures and technology that became available, and secondly because the internet was opened up for commercial use in 1992. But even before that, international collaboration between US, UK, and French researchers in the 1980s set the scene. Particularly significant was the work of young British computer scientist and internet idealist Tim Berners-Lee at CERN in Switzerland in the 1980s,[20] beginning with invention of the World Wide Web (WWW) in 1989, shortly followed by the WWW's Hypertext Transfer Protocol (HTTP)[21] and Hypertext Markup Language (HTML), both designed by Berners-Lee to facilitate communication (see Berners-Lee, 1999; Abbate, 1999; Cerf, 1993; Gillies & Cailliau, 2000). Berners-Lee's WWW browser developed in 1990, followed by other web browsers (e.g., Mosaic, in 1993, later called Netscape), led to the internet boom in the 1990s (see Figure 2).

---

[18] The transmission of data 'packets' in a digital network is a more efficient, reliable, and fault-tolerating way. Data is broken into suitably sized blocks for rapid transfer through routing by network devices to the destination.

[19] It helped that the computer industry was itself highly networked by the 1970s, with amateurs as well as professional programmers supplemented by a plethora of information scientists, librarians, and others geared to creating links between different computer communities as well as the public more generally (Driscoll, 2012).

[20] In his autobiography *Weaving the Web*, Berners-Lee (1999) describes his original vision for the World Wide Web as 'encompassing the decentralised, organic growth of ideas, technology and society', unfettered by 'the hierarchical classification systems into which we bound ourselves' (Berners-Lee, 1999: 1–2).

[21] The Hypertext Transfer Protocol (HTTP) is an application internet layer protocol suitable for distributed, collaborative, hypermedia information systems, such as the WWW. Using HTTP, hypertext documents can be linked and easily accessed by users through hyperlinks, that is, clicks or taps on screen in a web browser. It draws on a client–server model architecture whereby clients (service requestors) with unique IP addresses take user interactions and translate them into requests for services from servers (in the form of other computers, files, and databases) distributed in a communications network.

Figure 2 Tim Berners-Lee at the Science Museum for the Web@30 event, March 2019. Jwsluubbock via Wikimedia Commons, CC BY-SA 4.0.

2.5 Increased Focus on the User Experience and Preferences

The birth of the internet and its dramatic expansion facilitated by its underlying client–server model and distribution of content on different servers throughout the world, with the underlying technologies provided for free courtesy of Berners-Lee and CERN, brought content closer to individual users. With relative ease, individuals and user groups could easily learn the ropes of web programming to access content, that is, data/information databases and any other forms of data, such as images, videos, or web applications. The very first search engine, 'Archie', emerged a year after the WWW was launched, invented by the Bajan-Canadian computer programmer Alan Emtage (Samuel, 2017). The WWW provided a common way to access information on the internet through websites and helped to raise the popularity of the internet. From this time on, the internet's capacity expanded dramatically with the development of fibre-optic technology and the rollout of fibre-optic cables in the mid 90s, together with vast improvements in search engine optimisation. These developments revolutionised commerce, culture, and technology, and within a short period of time the commercial world capitalised on the rise of the internet, giving users the ability to navigate and search the Web. The Google search engine was founded in 1998, based on Larry Page and Sergey Brin's idea for this in 1995. Soon, a new world of internet banking and e-commerce opened in the early 1990s, with the first online item sold in 1994. (According to Dan Kohn,

Sting's CD *Ten Summoner's Tales*, including the two famous songs, 'Shape of my Heart' and 'Fields of Gold', was the first item that was bought online, on 11 August 1994; Lewis, 1994.) With the growth in interconnectivity between many different networks and network points, network service providers started to offer network access to commercial customers. The 1990s is also labelled as the second generation of digital cellular technology, launched in Finland, which gave rise to mobile phones and smartphones becoming the dominant personal accessory and business tool at the time. Since this time, there has been an overwhelming era of competition in the development and progress of mobile phones and supportive networking (wireless) infrastructures.

Parallel to these developments, earlier forms of social networking activities commenced in the 1970s and 1980s, first with the development of nascent forms of interaction and communication in the form of online chats, message forum applications, and bulletin board systems. These focused mainly on interaction between work-related groups and colleagues using early message forums and online chat room applications, which soon evolved to new forms of interaction allowing users to search and find content. For example, in 1990 Classmates.com was launched, which helped current school classmates find and contact each other online – making yearbooks of more than 30 million people available (i.e., 90,000 yearbooks from over 200,000 high schools). For the first time user groups could interact with websites to search and retrieve content from large databases. With these early forms of interaction, searching and retrieving content formed the basis for the development of social media applications in the mid to late 1990s (e.g., Myspace and Facebook), with blogging and instant messaging gaining popularity in the 2000s onwards. Of course, these networks quickly shifted to a business model which depended on a high degree of personal data processing, not all of it fully transparent and trustworthy. For its more idealistic creators and users, it was a far cry from the original ideal of a networked technology for free information-sharing enabling positive social connections and collaborations and, in the words of Berners-Lee (1999), 'support[ing] and improv[ing] our weblike existence in the world' (123).

User interactions with applications dramatically improved the user experience when interacting in networks, leading to the development of the discipline called human–computer interaction (HCI) (also from the 1980s onwards), which concentrates on how humans interact with computers. This discipline, which 'represents the convergence of several distinct yet related fields: human factors, management information systems, computer engineering, cognitive psychology, computer science, design, and social science, among others' (Gorichanaz & Venkatagiri, 2021: 391), has significantly shaped user research, user experience design, and the development of user interfaces of computing applications that collect, retrieve, and provide access to data. Initially its particular focus was efficiency and ease of use, but in more recent years this has expanded to encompass the treatment of data protection/data privacy, treating these as equally part of the user experience. Thus, while before the 2000s discussions about incorporating human preferences for data protection/data privacy into the design of computer systems and practices were sparse, that began to change in the second and third generation of HCI. Even so, as visionary HCI scholars Mark Ackerman and Scott Mainwaring (2005) noted in the early 2000s, there is more work to be done in terms of HCI's accommodation of data rights – pointing to the need for further cross-cultural studies of 'privacy', more research geared to 'understanding of the diversity and complexity of user preferences, and potential clusterings' (as part of a broader program of HCI research on individual differences), along with more consideration of 'visualizations and intelligent tutoring systems for privacy, in a range of applications' (Ackerman & Mainwaring, 2005: 400). While much has gone on in the decades since Ackerman and Mainwaring penned this advice, I would add that work still needs to be done, including addressing particular problems raised by the internet and other communications networks and systems through which information flows. Much of my work in recent years has focused on designing for human–computer interaction around data protection/data privacy in these contexts (see, for example, Bosua et al., 2019; Bosua et al., 2023).

2.6 Implications for Data Rights

The internet pioneers were focused on making the internet free and accessible to everyone. But it did not take long for the escalating breakthroughs in the design and proliferating uses of user interfaces, innovative hardware, and networking technologies from the early 1990s to raise concerns about data protection/data privacy, even in the computing community. This was also a period of development of some major new laws, with Europe – rather than the US – leading the way here with its 1995 EU Data Protection Directive (European Union, 1995), the precursor to the General Data Protection Regulation of 2016 (European Union, 2016), as discussed in more detail in Section 3. Certainly, I would say that even in Europe, where I have lived and worked most recently, the computing and legal disciplines have not, as yet, forged a united front that is focused on the rights of data subjects. However, as canvassed in this section, the divisions were greater prior to 2000, with no indications that the computing and legal disciplines 'spoke the same language' (see, for example, Karas, 2002a, 2002b; Solove, 2002). And the idealism, such as it was, in computer science circles was chiefly centred on free information sharing. In the words of Berners-Lee, who has subsequently become a leading voice on data protection/data privacy (including in the formulation of industry standards),[22] '[t]he individual was [seen as] incredibly empowered' at the beginning, adding: 'that empowerment is something we've lost' (Brooker, 2018).

3 Jing Qian and Megan Richardson, From Pragmatism to Activism

3.1 Introduction

As the earlier sections of this Element have detailed, faced with the felt need to regulate proliferating and increasingly computerised and automated data processing practices, a common legal policy response was a bureaucratic set of legal standards regarding the processing of personal data, with lawmakers often working closely in hand with industry professionals. In this section we consider how these legal standards were formulated with significant input also from some notable post-war pragmatists like Alan Westin (Law Professor at Columbia University and author of several notable empirical studies on current practices and attitudes), Spiros Simitis (Professor of Labour Law, Civil Law, and Legal Informatics at the University of Frankfurt, and later the first data protection commissioner for the state of Hesse, in West Germany), and Michael Kirby (already in the 1970s the deputy president of the Australian Conciliation and Arbitration Commission, later becoming a distinguished law reformer and judge, and chief architect of OECD standards in 1980). We argue that, while experience of the internet has more recently helped to galvanise a public activism movement for data rights across the board, encompassing even some of those in industry circles (including idealistic computer scientists like Tim Berners-Lee, as noted in Sections 2.4 and 2.5), we can see the roots of this social movement in the 1980s, even before the internet had fully emerged. Indeed, the

---

[22] Berners-Lee was instrumental in setting up the World Wide Web Consortium (W3C) which compiles a set of best practice standards for Web development languages, architectures and services for the WWW. The consortium provides standards that are based on fairness, openness, royalty-free 'we make the web work for everyone' principles for W3C compliance. The most recent W3C standards are the Web Content Accessibility Guidelines (WCAG) 2.1, of 21 September 2023. Designed to ensure compliance with national data protection/data privacy standards (e.g., the EU General Data Protection Regulation's requirement for explicit consent), this standard serves as an international baseline design standard. But W3C is not the only standard-setting organisation, and perhaps not even the most ambitious. The Institute for Electronical Engineers (IEEE), founded in 1963, is a US-based professional body for electronics and electrical engineers and other related computing disciplines. The IEEE standards community includes thought leaders and technical experts throughout the world coming from industry, academia, research and development organisation, governments, and civil society organisations. The IEEE is working towards standards for ethically aligned design with the focuses on human well-being with autonomous and intelligent systems as the priority.

West German Census Act Case (1983), which led the West German Constitutional Court to proclaim a right to 'informational self-determination', has all the hallmarks of what would later become a pattern of data rights activism pushing for an expansive treatment of data rights as civil rights and human rights in years to come.

One thing that was evident in this period was that there were significant changes taking place in understandings of data rights. And, we argue, these changes extended to the basic character of data rights as *rights*. Thus while data rights were initially presented as a fairly limited set of bureaucratic legal rights regarding the processing of personal data that corresponded to legal obligations on those responsible for the processing, as with early data protection regimes, by the 1980s they started to be seen as both civil rights designed to empower rights subjects and human rights grounded in ideas of human dignity and liberty. Whether these latter rights were termed 'data protection' rights, or 'data privacy' rights, or simply 'privacy' rights, it was the same – these terms meaning much the same when it comes to discussions of rights over personal data entailed in data processing (cf. Bygrave, 2014: xxv). Further, much of the major development that occurred in this period took place outside the official realm of international human rights texts, their interpretations and applications – although ultimately, to some extent, these followed the line. At the same time, pragmatism did not disappear completely as activism became more powerful: even by the end of the period, the influence of pragmatism remained strong, with its ideologies of mediation and compromise to achieve practical outcomes reflected in concepts like 'proportionality' in legal formulations of data rights even as civil rights and human rights.

3.2 Policy Pragmatists and Bureaucratic Rights

In 1980, the expert group charged with framing the *OECD Guidelines on the Protection of Privacy and Transborder Flows of Personal Data* noted that, '[o]f the OECD Member countries more than one-third have so far enacted one or several laws which, among other things, are intended to protect individuals against abuse of data relating to them and to give them the right of access to data with a view to checking their accuracy and appropriateness', with others actively contemplating similar reforms to their laws (OECD, 1980: 24). Moreover, the expert group continued, certain common basic principles could be identified as 'elementary components' of 'the area of protection':

> Some core principles of this type are: setting limits to the collection of personal data in accordance with the objectives of the data collector and similar criteria; restricting the usage of data to conform with openly specified

purposes; creating facilities for individuals to learn of the existence and contents of data and have data corrected; and the identification of parties who are responsible for compliance with the relevant privacy protection rules and decisions. (OECD, 1980: 24)

These principles, once synthesised and refined into OECD principles by the expert group, received backing as international standards by an OECD Council resolution in September 1980 (see OECD, 1980: 11–12). The Council of Europe's (1981) Convention for the Protection of Individuals with Regard to Automatic Processing of Personal Data (Convention 108) endorsed similar standards a year later, as did the first EU Data Protection Directive (European Union, 1995) fifteen years later – albeit with slightly more stringent standards for sensitive, or 'special', data, including data as to race, political or religious opinions, health or sexual life) (Council of Europe, 1981: Article 6; European Union, 1995: Article 8), along with other improvements in terms of the level and scope of protection. Another five years later, the Article 8 'right' to data protection in the EU Charter of Fundamental Rights would be framed as a right 'founded on the indivisible, universal values of human dignity, freedom, equality and solidarity' (European Union, 2000, 2007: Preamble). As specified in Article 8(2), '[s]uch data must be processed fairly for specified purposes and on the basis of the consent of the person concerned or some other legitimate basis laid down by law' (European Union, 2000, 2007: Article 8(2)). Further of relevance is the general limitation on the scope of Charter rights in Article 52, stating that '[s]ubject to the principle of proportionality, limitations may be made only if they are necessary and genuinely meet objectives of general interest recognised by the Union or the need to protect the rights and freedoms of others' (European Union, 2000, 2007: Article 52). However, as Bart van der Sloot (2017) posits, 'not only does a general limitation clause apply ..., the fundamental right to data protection is in itself already a compromise between different legitimate interests' (22). How did it come to this? A human right that seems neither revolutionary nor grandly humanistic, for all its focus on human values: a right designed for good bureaucratic systems in a society which places a high but not absolute value on human freedom? A right that, for all its activist origins, is still quite pragmatic.

One reason, we suggest, was the prevailing ethos of pragmatism that characterised the early data protection/data privacy laws noted by the OECD expert group and discussed in more detail in earlier sections of this Element, setting in train the later developments noted above. Note that we are using the term 'pragmatic' here in the general sense put forward by William James in the nineteenth century, of searching for mediatory positions that will allow for practical solutions to 'actual-world' problems, and resisting over-reliance on extremes of different philosophies and styles of reasoning (James, 1907; cf. Lindblom, 1959).[23] In short, we argue, pragmatists like Westin and Simitis (and later Kirby) resisted the extremes of Weberian-style rationalist reasoning that, in a rational bureaucracy, the bureaucratic subject would be regarded as subservient to the demands of a well-designed and functioning bureaucratic machine whose expertise was the processing of data. But they did not advocate for high-level civil rights or human rights for data subjects. Rather, they supported the development of important but nevertheless quite limited data subjects' rights, designed to enable 'fair' practices of data processing to continue. By and large, their principal concern was to achieve the establishment and operation of a rather limited set of positive legal rights for data processing subjects (coming with correlative duties) which would shape rather than cede power to data subjects themselves.

Consider, for instance, the genesis of the Hessian data protection law of 1970 (Hesse, 1970), considered in more detail in Section 1.2. On the 45th anniversary of this law, its architect, Spiros Simitis, in an interview with journalist Bernd Frye at Goethe University (see Simitis, 2015), explained the principal impetus for the new law as lying in the recognised need to provide an adequate system of regulation for the collection and uses (and other processing) of personal data, giving as an example automated data processing of patient data at hospitals which were then being built in the Federal Republic. Generally this was seen by the government as allowing for more efficient diagnosis and treatment. But it came in a period of intense public debate about automated data processing, with hospital data processing a significant instance. As Simitis elaborates, he was invited by the Hessian government to draft a proposal for regulation and, following government scrutiny and some modifications made from the government side, the draft was put to the parliament and approved: The first data protection legislation in the world had come into being. This is hardly the stuff of a civil or human right to data protection. Likewise, as discussed further in Section 1.2, the regimes that came after the Hessian law in the 1970s were essentially designed to deal with practical problems rather than being framed as

---

[23] James uses the terms 'tough-minded' versus 'tender-minded' to explain the extremes that he saw the pragmatist as needing to work through in the US at the turn of the twentieth century. But, as Margaret Jane Radin (1989: 1714) points out, he uses 'tough-minded' not in the sense we might today of rationalistic in an economic, especially Chicagoan sense, but rather as referencing deeply empirical approaches, with more theoretical 'rationalistic' approaches identified as 'tender-minded' (see, for example, James, 1907: 11-12). On the other hand, by the 1950s, Charles Lindblom, who also advocated for a pragmatic approach (and argued it was the approach policy-makers generally adopted), suggests that the extreme positions of the time which the pragmatist needed to mediate between did not entail sharp distinctions between of rationalist and empirical approaches, but rather reflected different 'ideological' positions (for instance, conservative vs. liberal: Lindblom, 1959: 83). In this Element we use the term 'pragmatic' to denote mediating positions in the current context.

civil rights and human rights (albeit with the partial exception of the French law of 1978, with its language of information technology being in the service of the citizen and protection regarding automated decision-making).

Even in the US, where the language used was 'privacy' rather than 'data protection', it was clear that what was being talked about was a pragmatic system of data protection. Westin was one of those instrumental in the development of a new extended meaning of 'privacy' being adopted in the US, stating in *Privacy and Freedom* (1967) that 'privacy' in the context of data processing encompasses 'the claim of individuals, groups or institutions to determine for themselves when, how, and to what extent information about them is communicated to others' (Westin, 1967: 7), along with contiguous entitlements 'to be notified when information is put into key central files[,] ... to examine the information that has been put into ... [their] file, to challenge its accuracy in some kind of administrative proceeding (with court review), and to submit a reply or explanation that would be coupled permanently to the information' (325). Yet, in keeping with his pragmatic approach, this extended meaning was offered as (at most) an incremental development of older meanings of privacy, as concerned essentially with private life. Further, Westin suggested that pragmatic solutions would be sufficient to satisfy the concerns of the American public which by the late 1960s thought that 'large-scale data collection and processing of information about individuals and groups' were 'serious problems involving technology and privacy' (Westin, 1967: 321). Indeed, in his later survey work, from the late 1970s, Westin categorised the majority of Americans, according to his surveys, as 'privacy pragmatists', as distinct from 'privacy fundamentalists' and 'privacy unconcerned', defining these as people 'who, while concerned about privacy, will sometimes trade it off for other benefits' (see Kumaraguru & Cranor, 2005: 4; Hoofnagle & Urban, 2014).

That Westin's work was significant in the formulation of the US Privacy Act 1974 has been noted already in Section 1.2. After *Privacy and Freedom*, Westin and Michael Baker, a sociologist at Brooklyn College of the City University of New York, published their report, *Databanks in a Free Society; Computers, Record-Keeping, and Privacy* (Westin & Baker, 1972), which (according to their summary, published a year later) set out to provide 'the first nation-wide, factual study of what the use of computers is actually doing to recordkeeping processes in the United States, and what the growth of large-scale databanks, both manual and computerized, mean for the citizen's constitutional rights to privacy and due process' (Westin & Baker, 1973: 25).[24] Westin and Baker's

---

[24] The report also noted the protections available, or being discussed, to address similar concerns in other jurisdictions and made particular reference to the Hessian data protection regime as a regime that provided data protection standards for state government databanks under the

(1973) report concluded that the significant problem with record keeping from the public's perspective, amplified by the efficiencies of computerised record keeping, was the use of personal records to 'control the rights, benefits and opportunities of Americans' (28). The report pointed both to difficulties with the criteria used to make such judgements ('religious, racial, political, cultural, sexual, educational, etc.'), and 'the procedures by which the decisions are reached, especially those that involve secret proceedings and prevent individuals from having access to records about them' (28). But its authors focused especially on the second in their proposals for bureaucratic standards, designed to provide 'proper safeguards for privacy and due process, and create mechanisms for public scrutiny and review' (28). They also referenced the US Fair Credit Reporting Act of 1970, with its standards for credit consumer reports impacting subjects' eligibility for credit, jobs, and insurance, etc. Under that Act, consumer reporting agencies are obliged to ensure that credit histories are accurate and relevant, and subjects are allowed the right to inspect their credit records and to request corrections; but the collection of sensitive data is not precluded, as civil liberty groups had sought (Editorial Board, *Minnesota Law Review*, 1972: 838). Recent US scholars have noted how the Privacy Act and the Fair Credit Reporting Act fit the 'consumer protection' model of data protection/data privacy protection in the US (Chander et al., 2021). But the more general point to be made here is that they also follow the pragmatic mode favoured by scholars such as Westin.

The same pragmatic influence from Kirby and his expert group can be seen in the OECD (1980) guidelines. As Kirby later pointed out, the OECD principles were designed to 'promote the harmonization of domestic privacy laws' that could work across national borders (see Kirby, 1983: 199–200; Kirby, 2011). Of course, as we have been arguing, these laws were already quite pragmatic, so harmonising was unlikely to rise above that. Indeed, the 1980 OECD report reads as a pragmatic statement on the value of harmonised data protection/data privacy standards for business and trade, even while noting the need to pay attention to 'rights' in elaborating its principles and requiring that member states should 'provide for reasonable means for individuals to exercise their rights' (OECD, 1980: (19)). The same can be said of the Council of Europe's Convention 108 explicitly premising its intent as '[r]ecognising that it is necessary to reconcile the fundamental values of the respect for privacy and the free flow of information between peoples', as well as 'increasing flow across frontiers of personal data

---

aegis of the data protection commissioner (at that time still Simitis) – although noting that any regulatory approach adopted in the US would need to pay heed to 'the particular (and often very different) legal and political conditions' of the United States (Westin & Baker, 1972, 493), in particular the 'American commitment to civil liberties' (Westin & Baker, 1972, 405).

undergoing automatic processing' (Council of Europe, 1981: Preamble). Kirby (1983) explains the pragmatic position guiding these international legal harmonisation regimes of the early 1980s: 'it is helpful to have an internationally agreed statement of "basic rules". They provide an intellectual framework for local laws. As technology makes different legal jurisdictions more interdependent, it is inevitable that closer attention will be needed in the future to practical international efforts at harmonization of laws' (2000).

Some have suggested that a particular reason for the qualified terms of the national and transnational legal standards of the 1970s and the early 1980s was that those advocating for and adopting more stringent standards were still in the realm of 'the fear and risk of abuses' rather than actual abuses, which might have strengthened the case for forceful demands for a civil right, let alone human right, to data protection (see Hondius, 1975: 7–8). At least that was the position of some of the bureaucrats involved in formulating the standards. For instance, Frits Hondius, legal adviser at the Secretariat General of the Council of Europe, in his 1975 study of emerging data protection law in Europe, quotes the view of Gerhard Stadler (chairman or member of various expert groups in the Council of Europe and in the OECD) that for those advocating for change the approach was one of 'fighting against windmills which have not yet been built' (Hondius, 1975: 8; cf. Stadler & Herzog, 1982: 5). If so, this was soon to change, and in the country with the most immediate memory of extremes of abusive wartime data processing.

3.3 Transition to Civil Rights and Human Rights

The West German Census Act Case (1983) reflects the public response to the Federal Census Act of 1983, which provided for the collection of comprehensive data (including quite sensitive data) on persons situated within the Federal Republic of Germany, including name, address, sex, marital status, religion, sources of income, housing, employment, and educational background. Further, the anticipated expanded use of computers to collect and process this information heightened the tension about the proposed census as a totalitarian regime in the eyes of those complaining and ultimately bringing the case. In sum, according to historian Larry Frohman, the formalised objections amounted to some 102 formal complaints and 1,121 less formal petitions, which in the proceedings were brought together with arguments of lawyers and data protection commissioners (including Simitis, as the Hessian data protection commissioner) about the risks of unrestricted data processing (Frohman, 2012: 357–358).[25]

---

[25] Frohman (2012) notes that '[m]ost of the privacy commissioners continued to maintain that the legitimate concerns regarding census data could be met by the organisational precautions.

Although the Federal Data Protection Act of 1977 was already in place before the proposed census roll-out, it was clearly regarded as insufficient to safeguard data subject rights in the way sought in this case (Hornung & Schnabel, 2009: 86). As the West German Constitutional Court elaborated, 'the individual must be protected from the unlimited collection, storage, use and transmission of personal data as a condition of free personality development under modern conditions of data processing', premising this on the basic rights to dignity and free development of personality in Articles 1 and 2 of the post-war Constitution (BVerfG, 1983: 410). More specifically, 'an individual's right to plan and make decisions and without pressure or influence from others' needs to be guarded from unpredictable sharing of personal data 'in a given area of ... [the individual's] social environment' (BVerfG, 1983: 410). Not surprisingly, given the context of the case and the boldness of the court's reasoning, the social ramifications of the decision were greater than its strict legal consequences – which in the words of Donald Kommers and Russell Miller were merely 'to strike down three minor provisions of the 1983 statute' (Kommers & Miller, 2012: 411). After the case, the protests did not go away, resurfacing in 1987 (see Figure 3), when the government again attempted to mount a national census (in modified form). By then, the West German Constitutional Court's identification of a right to

Figure 3 Protest gegen die Volkszählung 1987: Bcklebung der Berliner Mauer mit Personenbögen. Florian-schäffer (Originaltext: eigene Fotografie), via Wikimedia Commons, CC BY-SA 3.0.

Simitis, however, went further than other colleagues in criticising the law, and he supported the call for a temporary injunction, though he remained a staunch defender of the need for such statistics' (358) for social planning purposes.

'informational self-determination' in 1983 was an emboldening force on the protestors' side – despite later courts' reluctance to entertain the 'fundamental challenges' they might seek to raise (Hannah, 2017: 178).

According to German social theorist Jürgen Habermas, what made the Census Act Case significant was that the foundations of the right to informational self-determination were a direct public response to the still-remembered 'twentieth-century moral catastrophe' of the Nazi regime (Habermas, 2010: 465). Moreover, as Frohman argues, the census protests and ultimately the case had as much to do with the rapid increase of information technologies in governmental management practice and well-considered fears about the effects for civil liberties in this highly developed modern state (Frohman, 2012: 336). Certainly, from the perspective of the court, the immediate purpose of its articulation of a new right to informational self-determination was to offer a definite response to one of the major challenges of digital society in the 1980s, namely the risks (for humans) of new invasive technologies, impeding the individual's prospects of self-development for the individual's good and, what is more, 'the common good, because self-determination is an elementary functional condition of a free democratic community based on its citizens' capacity to act and participate' (BVerfG, 1983: 410). These realities provided the context and backdrop for a right to informational self-determination which is framed by the court in the Census Act Case as both as a civil right (designed to empower citizens in the face of technologised state power) and a human right, premised on the fundamental rights to dignity and free development of personality in the post-war West German Constitution. Thus, in the words of Habermas, the mid-century West German constitutional rights to dignity and free development of personality were now, in the 1980s, being called on to address new conditions that had 'merely made us aware of something that was inscribed in human rights implicitly from the outset – the normative substance of the equal dignity of every human being' (Habermas, 2010: 467).

At the same time, Habermas offers a rejoinder to concerns raised by his contemporary Niklas Luhmann, that, with a broadening of human rights in modern times to deal with current social ills, the inflation of their symbolic medium 'ruins' their 'value', in that as human rights have become too ideological and too unrealistic, 'it begins to appear normal that human rights will not be taken seriously' (Luhmann, 2004: 485). Specifically, Habermas suggests that the realism of the right to informational self-determination comes from its character as essentially a pragmatic right (i.e., per James, one that is designed for practical effect and resists the extremes of utopian philosophies and styles of reasoning) – even notwithstanding the utopian-sounding language of a 'right to informational self-determination'. Such rights, 'hav[ing] the form of enforceable subjective rights that grant specific liberties and claims', are 'designed to be spelled out in concrete terms through democratic legislation, to be specified from case to case in adjudication, and to be enforced in cases of violation ... [and] circumscribe precisely that part (and only that part) of morality which can be translated into the medium of coercive law and become political reality in the robust shape of effective civil rights' (Habermas, 2010: 470). Thus, although the right to 'informational self-determination' may properly be viewed as a product and instrument of civil rights activism, its pragmatism in the hands of the West German Constitutional Court and the legislature (both in Germany and, more broadly, across the EU when it came to framing data protection standards)[26] has allowed this right to transcend the 'deceptive images of a social utopia that guarantees collective happiness' (Habermas, 2010: 476) in aid of a more realistic yet desirable set of outcomes.

3.4 Data Rights as Responsive and Pragmatic

Arguably, what we see in the *Census Act* (1983) case of the early 1980s, with its civil rights activism balanced by pragmatism in the hands of court and legislature, is a shift towards what sociologists Philip Selznick and Philippe Nonet refer to as 'responsive law' (Nonet & Selznick, 1978) – treating 'social pressures as sources of knowledge' (77) in aid of 'civil morality' (16) and social 'participation' (16). Indeed, as these authors suggest, responsiveness encourages a 'sophisticated pragmatism in the spirit of John Dewey, which regards [government and other policy] ends as problematic and subject to reconstruction in light of their costs' (Nonet & Selznick, 1978: 85; cf. Cohen-Eliya & Porat, 2010: 278). And ideally the rights produced can become engrafted with an institutionalised legal dimension that even Luhmann can approve (see also Verschraege, 2002: 263).

Likewise, we can see a certain responsiveness in the UN Human Rights Committee's (1988) expansive 'interpretation' in its Official Comment no. 16 of the Article 17 right to privacy in the International Covenant on Civil and Political Rights (UN General Assembly, 1966); in the expansive treatments by

---

[26] An example is the principle of proportionality that the West German Constitutional Court in the *Census Act* case identified, noting that the individual must 'accept certain limits on the right to informational self-determination for reasons of compelling public interest', while the legislature 'must observe the principle of proportionality, limiting the individual's right 'only to the extent necessary for the protection of public interests' (Census Act Case, 1983: 410). As to the principle of proportionality in the EU Charter of Fundamental Rights (European Union, 2000, 2007), see Sections 3.2 and 4.3.

the European Court of Human Rights of the European Convention on Human Rights Article 8 right to private life (Council of Europe, 1950), for example in cases of searches and seizures/surveillance initiated by individuals and civil society groups (such as *Niemietz v. Germany* (1992); *Copland v. United Kingdom* (2007); *Big Brother Watch and Others v. the United Kingdom* (2021)); and in the right to 'the protection of personal data' in Article 8 of the EU Charter (European Union, 2000, 2007) – the last a right inspired by the right to informational self-determination (Lynskey, 2014: 591), which in the arguments of claimants and interpretations of judges has moved beyond a narrow right to '[fair processing] for specified purposes on the basis of consent of the person concerned or some other legitimate basis laid down by law' (European Union, 2000, 2007: Article 8(2)), as discussed in Section 4.

4 Damian Clifford, Making and Remaking Data Protection

4.1 Introduction

The legitimacy of the focus on 'control rights' in data protection/data privacy laws appears to be increasingly under strain, or at least according to some observers. Control is, as Margot Kaminski notes, a term that a groundswell of 'scholars now love to hate' (Kaminski, 2022: 391). The core of this critical view of data protection law centres on the belief that individual control is a fallacy and one that damages the interests of individuals and society as we, the data subjects, are neither best placed nor capable of acting in our own interests and that data controllers take advantage of this, effectively doing what they want, due to limited enforcement. Thus the focus turns to power. The criticisms have been particularly prevalent in the recent US scholarship. Daniel Solove, for instance, argues that although control has value, a legislative approach that focuses on this simply allows policymakers to 'pat themselves on the back and claim that they did something to protect privacy, but they merely [send] people on a doomed quest' (Solove, 2023: 985; and generally Solove, 2025). Moreover, according to Julie Cohen (2021), '[a]tomistic, post hoc assertions of individual control rights … cannot meaningfully discipline networked processes that operate at scale'; and '[n]or can they reshape earlier decisions about the design of algorithms and user interfaces'. Indeed, Ezra Waldman (2022: 99) posits that there should be less focus within privacy laws on how individuals feel their personal data should be protected and more on how laws could be framed to achieve 'the collective goal of democratic governance' of the information economy. As a European data rights scholar, I believe that while we should pay attention to these concerns, they should not be treated as justification for rejection of the value of control rights as a central policy tool.

Specifically, I argue that data subjects' rights of control over their personal data should ideally be understood, interpreted, and applied as tools of data subject empowerment, both individually and collectively. On this reading, they are – or at least should be – concerned with much more than 'doomed' individual acts of consent, rather having broadly to do with ensuring 'the realization of freedom or autonomy' (Roessler, 2017: 190) of data subjects, or what might be termed 'normative agency' (Griffin, 2008: 45). At the same time, they need to take into account the challenges and affordances of current socio-technical contexts and circumstances – and respond to the pressures of new socio-technical control mechanisms that operate 'at scale'. As such, they are properly to be regarded as civil rights as well as human rights, underpinned by ideas of human dignity and liberty. Among other benefits of understanding data rights in this way is that the focus can then be squarely on their ability to unite and inspire data rights activism seeking empowerment and change, as well as emboldening more pragmatic efforts to specify, enforce, and supplement data rights in heterogeneous practical 'real-world' situations.[27] The EU General Data Protection Regulation 2016 (GDPR; European Union, 2016) offers an example of a modern rights-based law that roughly fits this mould. Nor should this be surprising, given it is designed to give effect to the right to data protection in Article 8 of the EU Charter of Fundamental Rights (European Union, 2000, 2007), making this not just a desirable but a legally necessary approach in the EU. As discussed elsewhere in this Element, the process began earlier, well before the Charter was framed and came into effect, and there are examples also outside the EU. But the GDPR has gone furthest (to date) in offering intellectually robust and practically important support for the efforts of diverse individuals and communities seeking to exercise normative agency in an increasingly datafied society.

4.2 Loss of Control and Rise of Control Rights

Control rights have long been an important part of data protection law even if there is variation in terms of how they are included. But one thing that is clear is that they are not just to be understood as rights to consent (or not). For example, in the early 1980 OECD guidelines, individual participation was included as a specific principle (OECD, 1980: 13)) as supplemented by the openness principle, which, in simple terms, encourages transparency. These principles remain in the current version (OECD, 2013). In contrast, in the Council of Europe's 1981 Convention 108, there was no specific reference to individual participation as a principle, but instead Article 8 included '[a]dditional

---

[27] See my book (Clifford, 2024) for further elaboration of these ideas.

safeguards for the data subject'. Despite the variations in the manner in which the rights are provided, however, there is substantive similarity in the control rights provided, which may be summarised as: a right to be informed and to access personal data in addition to the right have it corrected/rectified or deleted.

This list of rights has since been expanded significantly. For instance, newer data protection laws such as the Data Protection Directive in 1995 (European Union, 1995), and now the GDPR (European Union, 2016), the various consumer privacy Acts adopted at the state level in the US (most notably the California Consumer Privacy Act (2018)/California Privacy Rights Act (2020)), and the modernised Convention 108+ of 2018 (Council of Europe (2018), updating the original Convention 108 of 1981, amongst many others, have framed or emphasised new types of rights, going beyond or engrafting onto existing rights. Further, in addition to those control rights in the original Convention 108, Convention 108+ includes the right not to be subject to automated decision-making, the right to object, the right to have a remedy following violations of rights, and the right to assistance from a supervisory authority in exercising their rights (Council of Europe, 2018: updated Article 9). The expansion of the list of rights provided by these frameworks broadly maps those provided, first, in the EU Data Protection Directive 1995 and, now, in the more elaborate and expanded terms of the GDPR (see Figure 4), which provides the most comprehensive list of rights available.

As Kaminski (2022) observes, the sense that we have lost control of our personal data plays a significant part in the adoption of such control rights in data protection laws. As detailed earlier in this Element, data protection laws emerged in Europe at the national level in the 1970s and at the international level in the early 1980s. The adoption of the key international data protection law instruments – most notably, the OECD guidelines of 1980, and the Council of Europe's Convention 108, of 1981 – were then followed by another wave of national data protection law frameworks as well as the Data Protection Directive of 1995 (European Union, 1995), representing a first effort at harmonisation at the EU level. And citizens' fears of the loss of control over their personal data had much to do with the genesis of these early data protection laws, which allowed them a measure of control over the processing of their

Figure 4 Data subject rights in the EU General Data Protection Regulation (European Union, 2016).

personal data (even if this protection was watered down considerably in the making, with business and government actors, as well as pragmatic experts and law reformers, all playing a role here).

Likewise, this is also true in later developments in data protection law at the EU level from the 2010s. For example, Moritz Laurer and Timo Seidl (2021) argue that the Snowden revelations had a significant impact on the development of the GDPR. When the revelations started to appear in the media from 2013, the GDPR was already in the process of negotiation as the instrument to be adopted to replace the Data Protection Directive of 1995. And it was self-evident that it would be underpinned by the European Union's (2000) Charter of Fundamental Rights, which, with the Lisbon Treaty in 2007 (European Union, 2017) (in force from 2009), became part of the primary law of the reconstituted European Union. But the Snowden revelations had an impact on the political debate particularly in large EU member states such as Germany and France, producing a significant effect on shaping policymakers' attitudes to the reform process in the lead-up to the GDPR. In the words of Laurer and Seidl, the 'salience shock' the revelations produced 'saved' the GDPR from being watered down by establishment interests (Laurer & Seidl, 2021). In this environment, as in others, we can see that the value of a responsive data protection law as a way of addressing citizen fears was highly significant.

4.3 Institutionalising Data Rights: Objectives of EU Data Protection Law

Even so, data protection laws are clearly about more than data rights, and this was clear from their inception. Protection of individual rights is just one of the components of data protection frameworks, which also rely on a number of principles that aim at constraining the behaviour of controllers in order to ensure a *fairer* personal data processing environment (see Clifford & Ausloos, 2018; Clifford, 2024). This is not just on the side of users. For instance, the OECD principles of 1980 through to the EU Directive of 1995 (European Union, 1995) had a clear emphasis on promoting operational efficiency and efficient trade (see Bygrave, 2002: 160–164). And even with a more modern rights-based regime, as the GDPR (European Union, 2016) aspires to be, supported by the EU Charter of Fundamental Rights (European Union, 2000, 2007), there are other competing values underpinning the regime. In this respect, the GDPR is not a complete break with the earlier Directive.

In short, it is important to understand the history of the GDPR, with its roots extending back before the explicit recognition of a right to data protection in the EU Charter, as still relevant to conceptualising and understanding the GDPR today. With the Data Protection Directive of 1995, the EU legislator aimed to improve the functioning of the internal market by introducing a harmonised legal environment through the adoption of an EU instrument designed to eliminate disparities and therefore obstacles to free movement, reflecting its adoption under what is now Article 114 of the Treaty on the Functioning of the EU (TFEU; (European Union, 2008)). Article 114 of the TFEU constitutes the main treaty provision used to enact harmonisation measures. According to this provision, the European Union may adopt 'measures for the approximation of the provisions laid down by law, regulation or administrative action in Member States which have as their object the establishment and functioning of the internal market' (European Union, 2008: Article 114). This provision is thus not sector specific and does not grant the EU legislator any specific competence in relation to the adoption of secondary law for the protection of fundamental rights.

That is not to say that considerations of civil rights and human rights were excluded in the Directive of 1995. Even at the beginning, and independent of the internal market objective, the Directive was also viewed in some quarters as constituting a measure for the protection of fundamental rights. From the early 1970s onwards, the European Parliament had expressed its commitment to their protection (Lynskey, 2015: 50–51). However, despite the political will on the side of the European Parliament, and the fact that fundamental rights were viewed as protected as part of the constitutional fabric of the EU legal order, the Court of Justice remained reluctant to acknowledge this objective for the Directive, instead emphasising the market integration goal in its earliest rulings. In particular, the Court intimated, it was the intention of the Directive's measures to improve the functioning of the internal market, and to find otherwise would potentially undermine their value by requiring a case-by-case analysis of each circumstance. In both the *Rundfunk* (2003) and the *Lindqvist* (2003) decisions the Court took the view that a broader interpretation, taking account of fundamental rights standards, would render the application of the Directive uncertain, thus detracting from its harmonising objectives. The Court's approach here contrasted with the opinions of Advocate General Tizzano for both cases, who argued that, in the absence of a direct link with the internal market, the only possible justification for action would be the protection of fundamental rights (see *Randfunk*, 2003; *Lindqvist*, 2003). Yet the Court chose not to refer to the fundamental rights aspects outlined in the Advocate General's opinions on these cases. This perhaps, in part, relates to the fact that, irrespective of such considerations, it found that there was a link to the Directive's market integration basis, hence eliminating a need to analyse the fundamental rights objective argumentation thoroughly. Nevertheless, the omission more fundamentally suggested that (in the view of the Court) there was a lack of a general EU competence to adopt legislation on fundamental rights. As such it reflects something of the difficult history of the EU in terms of fundamental rights protection and the division of competence between the EU and its member states.[28]

Later this was to change, with the Court of Justice becoming more open to the idea of treating fundamental rights as a consideration lying at the root of the Directive. One trigger was the EU Charter of 2000, specifying in Article 8 that 'everyone has the right to the protection of personal data' (European Union, 2000: Article 8). But the Court's hesitancy about taking the lead in implementing this idea brought the market integration objective into question in subsequent judgments. Initially, in assessing the balancing of data protection and privacy with other rights, freedoms, and interests in cases such as *Satamedia* (2008) and *Promusicae* (2008), the Court awarded a large degree of discretion to member states in the application of this balancing exercise, thereby endangering the market integration goal which had been key in the earlier case law (Lynskey, 2015: 55–58). Nevertheless, there has been a strong signal in the later jurisprudence of the Court of Justice that fundamental rights have been considered in a new light since the adoption of the Lisbon Treaty in 2007 (European Union, 2017) (coming into force in 2009) and its designation of binding constitutional status upon the Charter. In particular, for instance the *Schecke & Eifert* (2010) ruling and the other subsequent judgments contrast strongly with the Court's previous rulings and provide adequate guidance to the national court in relation to the balancing process to be undertaken in the application of the principle of proportionality in the Charter – with the Court here 'meticulous[ly]' referencing the Charter (Lynskey, 2015: 64). This initial willingness to engage with Charter fundamental rights issues has continued and the Court has adopted a similarly robust approach in later high-profile judgments, such as: the 'right to be forgotten' case, *Google Spain SL & Google Inc. v. AEPD & Mario Costeja González* (2014); the data retention case, *Digital Rights Ireland Ltd v. Minister for Communications and Others* (2014); and the *Schrems I* (2015) and *Schrems II* (2020) cases, on cross-border data transfers. As these cases demonstrate, and as I will come back to, these judgments about data rights already show the important collective as well as individual dimensions of data rights.

They also show how the right to data protection in Article 8 of the Charter has taken on a life of its own. Initially, as Gráinne De Búrca (2001) explains, making the Charter part of the Lisbon Treaty of 2007, that is, the European Union's constitution, aimed at securing more popular legitimacy for the Union and

---

[28] Here one can refer to the famous *Solange II* (1986) case concerning the West German Constitutional Court. Also in terms of a lack of a positive duty to legislate as opposed to the negative duty not to breach fundamental rights which must be respected by the EU and its member states when they act within the scope of EU law.

a means of gathering support for existing EU activity. Even at its original adoption in 2000, the process of drafting the Charter was viewed as at least as important as the document which would emerge, in that the intention was not to create anything new substantively. In simple terms, the aim was to increase the visibility of something which already existed in EU law and to hence give fundamental rights a more prominent place in the process of European integration. After all, for the three decades prior to the initial drafting of the Charter, fundamental rights were protected as part of the constitutional fabric of the EU legal order in the form of an unwritten catalogue of rights constituting general principles of EU law.[29] However, despite the intention to merely raise popular awareness, the number of cases which mention the Charter, including those noted above, has dramatically increased since the coming into force of the Lisbon Treaty in December 2009, and its treatment has also become more robust. In hindsight, therefore, it is apparent that the attribution of binding force on the Charter has led to a significant change in the EU legal order and that, although initially presented as decorative rather than substantive in nature, in raising the profile of fundamental rights the Charter has forced the Union to take their protection more seriously, thereby pushing the Court of Justice in turn.

Nevertheless, although the EU is often seen as the flag-bearer of data rights, its standards are also directed by practical social and market-based concerns in the same way as the Directive, in keeping with the Union's socio-economic underpinnings. One reason is that, although the GDPR was adopted under a distinct legal basis (*viz.* Article 16 of the TFEU, inserted through the adoption of the Lisbon Treaty, rather than Article 114 of the TFEU, like the old Directive), this balance between rights protection and market making is still obvious. Article 16(1) of the TFEU repeats Article 8 of the Charter with its statement that '[e]veryone has the right to the protection of personal data concerning them' (European Union, 2008: Article 16(1)). Yet, importantly, Article 16(2) of the TFEU also specifies the EU legislature's competence with a specific reference to 'the free movement of such data' within the internal market. Hence, the use of Article 16 of the TFEU as the basis for the GDPR has

---

[29] Indeed, in the explanations to the Charter it is apparent that Article 8 was adopted on the basis of a series of other instruments, in particular the Data Protection Directive 95/46/EC (European Union, 1995), the Council of Europe (1981) Convention 108, and the right to private and family life, home and correspondence in Article 8 of the ECHR. For this as a not very coherent position, given the right to personal data protection had yet to be identified in those instruments (see González Fuster (2015)). Of course, this was also a time when there was a great deal of confusion about the relationship between the older right to privacy/private life and the newer right to data protection, and it was only later that it came to be accepted that data protection serves objectives beyond the protection of privacy/private life: see De Hert & Gutwirth (2009); Rodotà (2009); González Fuster & Gellert, (2012); Tzanou (2013); Kokott & Sobotta (2013); Lynskey (2015): 103–104; and Dalla Corte (2020).

not resulted in the removal of references to the importance of market integration.[30] Moreover, even with respect to its protection of data rights, we see the same pragmatic mediatory dimension to the GDPR's framing and operation of the right to data protection, giving effect to the Charter. In short, the Article 8 (rather qualified) right to data protection which forms the basis of the GDPR is not the only fundamental right or freedom to be considered where personal data are processed. Other Charter rights and freedoms along with interests may be relevant – for instance, the right to property, including intellectual property, the freedom to receive or impart information, and the freedom to conduct a business (see further, in this respect, Articles 11, 16, and 17 of the Charter and Article 1(2) of the GDPR, as analysed and balanced in cases like *Scarlet Extended v. SABAM* (2011) and *SABAM v. Netlog* (2012)). Further, as noted in Section 3.2, there is the general proportionality standard of Article 52 of the Charter.

In Section 4.4 I seek to push these ideas further to argue that the combination of a rigorous rights-based and a pragmatic mediatory approach is what makes the GDPR a particularly effective 'modern' instrument – and, if anything, this should be more explicitly asserted and vigorously addressed.

4.4 Social Impacts of Data Rights

The exercise of data subjects' rights of control over the processing of their personal data can certainly have broader societal impacts. But one feature of the GDPR (European Union, 2016) is how it has been specifically designed and deployed with social impact in mind. Thus, the GDPR explicitly goes beyond individual rights concerns in its effort to 'safeguard the collective social and cultural foundations which liberal democratic orders presuppose, and without which individual dignity, autonomy, and self-development would not be possible' (Yeung & Bygrave, 2021: 144). Karen Yeung and Lee Bygrave (2021) usefully point to features of the GDPR going beyond its 'fundamental rights' character in establishing a general regime regulating the processing of personal data, and extending, for instance, to compliance standards around data protection by design and impact assessments. I would go further to argue that even the rights themselves are framed and deployed in ways that promote social as well as individual ends – especially where these are taken up and pursued by data rights activists at the enforcement end. The *Google Spain* (2014) case is an example of a case initiated by a Spanish lawyer and 'everyday internet warrior' (Kassam, 2014), Mario Costeja González, supported by the *Agencia Española de Protección de Dato*s (AEDP), where the EU Court of Justice grappled with

---

[30] See further, for instance, recitals 2, 5, 7, 13, 21, 123, and 133 of the GDPR.

Figure 5 Max Schrems Bei den Big Brother Awards 2015 von Digitalcourage e. V. in Bielefeld. Fabian Kurz via Wikimedia Commons, CC-BY 4.0.

the true nature and meaning of the 'right of erasure' provided for in Article 12(b) of the EU Data Protection Directive (European Union, 1995), taking into account also the effect of Article 8 of the Charter. The Court's decision, in turn, formed part of the background for the framing of the 'right of erasure' in Article 17 of the GDPR. Likewise, in the *Schrems I* (2015) and *Schrems II* (2020) cases, instituted by activist Max Schrems (see Figure 5), the right of access in Article 15 of the GDPR (and Article 12 of the Directive) was used as a means of verifying compliance with the broader processing standards of the GDPR (cf. Ausloos, Mahieu & Veale 2019: 285). Although such examples do not mean that the rights provided in the GDPR are ideally framed,[31] they highlight that they serve both as a mechanism of individual choice and control, and also as means of holding controllers to account (cf. Quelle, 2018).

The same goes for features of the GDPR that are focused on compliance, such as the standards around data protection by design and impact assessments noted

---

[31] See, for instance, Article 22 of the GDPR's rather timid and obscure framing of a right not to be subject to automated decision-making, as critiqued *inter alia* by Guillermo Lazcoz and Paul De Hert (2023); Clifford et al. (2023).

above. As Yeung and Bygrave (2021) explain, these standards are central to the 'modern' forward-looking character of the GDPR. And, as I have argued elsewhere, the objectification of compliance standards ensures that the consequences are, by definition, societal (Clifford 2024). For example, failure to provide for 'the adoption of organisational and technical measures' that can give 'effective protection' against 'risk of abuse and against any unlawful access and use' (Clifford, 2024: 126), which the Court strongly hinted was needed for compliance with terms of the Charter's right to data protection in *Digital Rights Ireland* (2014: (40), (66)), would logically fall within the remit of Article 25 of the GDPR (see Bygrave, 2020: 575). Conversely, providing for effective protection measures should be of benefit not just to particular data subjects but for all of those affected by the data controller's practices. Likewise, where a data protection impact assessment required under Article 35 of the GDPR has not been conducted or has been conducted poorly in contravention of the requirements provided for in this Article, changes to the impact assessment process will be required for any future processing. Again, such examples reinforce the general point that even a data protection law that is framed largely in terms of effectively protecting fundamental data rights, as with the GDPR, can also have significant societal impacts.

4.5 Towards Structural Change: A Broader Role for Data Rights?

This is not to say that the core objections raised by the critical scholars noted at the beginning of Section 4 are completely invalid. As they usefully highlight, with their focus on power, there are information and power asymmetries, market effects, manipulative design practices, and cognitive capacity issues that affect the effective operation of a (control) rights-based data protection regime, especially where this is left in the hands of data subjects, imposing on them 'an endless burden of chores' that are incapable of being invoked in a systematic way and putting them at risk of being blamed for failing to exercise their rights with respect to 'hundreds if not thousands of organisations' (Solove 2023: 985; and see further Solove, 2024, who proposes supplemental protections of data subjects to bolster 'murky consent'). This may be a matter of particular concern for data protection regimes that rely on individuals for their enforcement, as for instance with the California Consumer Protection Act (2018), which, only now, with the passage of the California Privacy Rights Act (2020), been allocated an independent enforcement authority.[32] But, with the GDPR (European Union,

---

[32] Specifically, the California Privacy Protection Agency has authority to enforce the California Consumer Protection Act and prepare regulations to guide organisations in implementing it (with effect from 2023).

2016), where (like the Directive) provision is made for data protection authorities to carry out enforcement, these authorities can perform a useful role in this as in other contexts. For instance, I have argued that these authorities should be especially focused on violations of the GDPR at scale and how these affect society and, in particular, the interests of the most marginalised groups and interests (Clifford & Paterson, 2023). Likewise, as Claes Granmar points out, when it comes to big issues like 'the systematic checks of adequacy decisions' governing data transfers outside the EU, affecting the rights and interests not just of people in the EU but also in other parts of the world, EU data protection authorities will rightly likely be involved (Granmar, 2021: 65).

To date, regulatory enforcement of the GDPR has been a point of contention, with the data protection authorities in member states such as Ireland and Luxembourg receiving significant criticism regarding their perceived soft touch, thereby highlighting how cross-border personal data processing affects the resolution of disputes in the EU. Frustrations regarding some data protection authorities' perceived failure to enforce the GDPR have led to a noticeable tension between civil society organisations and the regulators. Again, this points to the value of such organisations and activists in not only bringing their own actions where authorities fail to act (as in the *Schrems* 2015 and *Schrems* 2020 cases) but also pushing authorities to act (as in the *Google Spain* (2014) case). And another important feature of the GDPR is the power of the European Data Protection Board (EDPB) to exercise authority over member state data protection authorities and bring them into line with a common European approach (as with the EDPB's 2023 binding decision on Meta data transfers pursuant to standard contractual clauses, instructing the Irish DPA to amend its draft decision to impose a fine on Meta for its systematic breaches of the GDPR: see EDPB, 2023). The recent landmark *Meta* (2023) case before the European Court of Justice also shows that not only data protection authorities but other authorities, such as in this case the German competition authority (*Bundeskartellam*) looking for effective remedies against Meta for exploiting its dominant market position in its treatment of its customers, may draw on and enforce the control rights in the GDPR – the court here interpreting Article 80 of the GDPR (which provides that rights can be enforced by a representative for one or more data subjects) broadly as covering the *Bundeskartellam*,[33] and agreeing with the *Bundeskartellam* that Facebook's reliance on contract and legitimate interests as conditions for lawful processing provided for in Article 6(1) (instead of consent) warranted scrutiny.

---

[33] See also (on the jurisdiction of a consumer protection authority, under Article 80 of the GDPR) *Meta* (2022).

Cases like *Meta* (2023) are promising in their implication that data rights embodied in a data protection regime can contribute to systemic regulation for the benefit of data subjects even beyond the strict confines of a data protection regime. Moreover, as we have shown in this Element, data rights themselves may exist outside a data protection regime – as for instance with rights to privacy/ private life provided for in international human rights texts, and (for that matter) the right to data protection in the EU Charter. And there may be other laws, as well, which make provision for data rights, such as the new EU Platform Workers Directive (European Union, 2024b) making provision for the right (of platform workers) not to be subject to automated decision-making in specific terms going beyond Article 22 of the GDPR (see Clifford et al., 2023). Even so, I accept that a modern data rights regime or set of regimes, for all its important social impacts, cannot fully account for and address all the potential collective harms that may result directly or indirectly from data processing technologies and practices – including the coercive and unequal structural characteristics of the modern information economy (see Zuboff, 2019; Cohen, 2019). Here competition and consumer laws, flexibly construed and adapted over time, may provide some recourse, as in the *Meta* (2023) case. More experimental attempts to address the challenges include provisions made for responsibilities of social media platforms and other digital services for information hosted and communicated via these platforms and services as with the EU Digital Services Act (European Union, 2023); and regulation of risky modern technologies as provided for in the EU Artificial Intelligence Act (European Union, 2024a) (see Lazcoz & de Hert, 2023).[34] As these indicate, laws going beyond data protection laws are clearly desirable and needed.

4.6 Review

To review, I have argued in this section that data subjects' rights of control over the processing of their personal data, being rights essentially of agency, play an important role in a well-designed modern data protection law like the GDPR (European Union, 2016), in the process engendering significant changes with societal benefits. Such rights and laws, therefore, are tools of individual and community empowerment in the information economy – although they can never cover the field entirely, at best coexisting with other laws. Although critical scholars may, in Kaminski's (2022) words, 'love to hate' control rights, I think hate is the easy route in that it fails to reflect the more complex reality and allows limited scope for improvement. On the other hand, I do not want to

---

[34] For more patchy AI regulation in the US (surviving a recent – failed – effort by Congress to limit State laws), see Hendrix & Lima-Strong (2025) and Pasquale (2025).

overclaim the benefits of relying on the GDPR for effective protection of data rights (cf. Lynskey, 2023). Rather, I have tried to plot a more nuanced picture, so that we can now turn to imagine a viable future for data rights.

Conclusion

Some say that fundamental rights are 'social constructs' (Yeung & Bygrave, 2021: 143). If so, modern data rights offer a particularly apt example. As mapped in this Element, their development was and continues to be embedded in the socio-technical conditions of the post-war twentieth century. Thus, it is impossible to view them as essentially 'natural' or 'transcendental' (even if that were possible for more ancient rights). Those established under the general rubric of data protection/data privacy may be understood as emerging in part out of the older right to privacy/private life identified in Article 12 of the Universal Declaration of Human Rights (UN General Assembly, 1948). But that right – important as it still is – offers a rather inadequate progenitor for the data rights established in response (*inter alia*) to computerised data processing systems and practices in the post-war decades. Yet, these were fought for and then accepted as civil rights and human rights to 'self-determination' (as the West German Constitutional Court put it in the Census Act Case (1983)). And, by the end of the period, they had moved well beyond the limited bureaucratic rights to transparency, access and information security, and so on, associated with 'fair information practices' in early data protection/data privacy regimes, which were quite widely accepted as necessary, including even by some of those on the government and industry side.[35] As argued in this Element, at best modern data rights (as exemplified, for instance, by the EU GDPR (European Union, 2016)) serve as effective tools of individual and community empowerment. Moreover, this is despite the reality that they are toned down in their legal institutionalisation and made subject to mediatory standards, reflecting the pragmatic idea that different rights, freedoms, and interests have to be accommodated in order to achieve practical outcomes, even for rights rooted in human dignity and liberty.

We can expect to see a lot more discussion and development of data rights in coming years, and even some new data rights, as new socio-technical challenges emerge, new fights for rights are taken up, and diverse communities and societies embrace and adapt the idea of data rights as a source of individual and community empowerment. Indeed, this is already occurring, including in the development of novel data rights outside the traditional Western settings of

---

[35] Although for some useful recommendations designed to make current versions of these types of rights (in particular, rights of transparency and access) relevant, effective, and constructive in the twenty-first century, see Pasquale (2025); and see also Thomas et al. (2022).

the UK, Europe, and the US (see, for example, Kukutai, Carroll & Walter, 2020; Kukutai, 2023). Moreover, even in more Western settings some new (or renewed) data rights emerging from current reform processes arguably transcend the now conventional legal data protection/data privacy regimes into which they may be thrust, taking on a character of their own as data rights. For instance, the right to be forgotten in Article 17 of the GDPR seems to fit with what Mathias Risse calls an 'epistemic right' (Risse, 2023), representing data subjects' contributions to the making of knowledge – including knowledge about their present and future aspirational selves (see Richardson, 2023a, ch. 4). And the right not to be subject to automated decision-making (which might better be termed a right of non-subjection to automated decision-making, reflecting its focus on the decision-making process) can be seen as part of a wider right of social dialogue, drawing as much on a tradition of industrial democracy as on data protection/data privacy norms (see Clifford et al., 2023).

Nevertheless, we suggest that more work needs to be done in reinventing data rights for the twenty-first century, where one of the ongoing overarching aims must be 'to prevent our societies from turning into societies of control, surveillance and social selection' under current socio-technical conditions (Rodotà, 2009: 82). Some examples of what we ideally would like to see, continuing and extending beyond themes touched on in this Element, include the following:

1. More looking across different frameworks for a panoply of data rights, which might include not just data protection/data privacy laws (as well as laws concerned more specifically with privacy/private life), but other laws, standards, and norms concerned with the generation, use, dissemination, etc. of data concerning humans, at the same time borrowing from/building on their ideas about how to make enforcement work (cf. Yeung & Bygrave, 2021; Clifford et al., 2023);
2. More appreciation of the value of different types of data rights as designed to address the different needs of diverse 'members of the human family' (UN General Assembly, 1948: Preamble; UN General Assembly, 1966: Preamble), including rights associated with increasingly ubiquitous cross-border data flows *inter alia* via social media platforms and digital services, as well as more consideration of ways to make such rights effective;
3. More readiness also to 'live with difference' in the treatment of data rights (Clifford, 2024; Clifford et al., 2022) – including different weightings of countervailing rights, freedoms, and interests (the European Court of Justice's rejection of a worldwide 'right to be forgotten' in the *Google v. CNIL* case (Google, 2019) may be an example here, although see point 4 below);

4. More care taken in distinguishing between genuine points of social and cultural difference and claims by elites that may not fully represent the views of society (cf., for instance, statements in the *CNIL* case noted above about the cultural value of free speech in the US versus surveyed public views in the US about the value of the right to be forgotten; as to which, see Auxier, 2020);
5. More focus on design of systems, standards, and laws to provide practically responsive support for data rights including in contexts of rapidly evolving socio-technical change (see Yeung & Bygrave, 2021; Lynskey, 2023) – which might include, for instance, recalibrating 'privacy/data protection by design' and other 'by design' approaches (see, for example, Bosua et al., 2019); and deploying data rights impact assessments for new technologies, systems, and programs with wide scope for public as well as expert participation (see Mantelero, 2022; Bosua et al., 2023);
6. More readiness to consider how data rights may have to change to accommodate socio-technical changes[36] – and whether they can provide the sole answer to every socio-technical change or are better to be considered as coexisting with other kinds of rights and regimes (cf. Kaminsky and Urban, 2021; De Hert, 2023), including new ones still to be developed.

---

[36] Including the traditional right to privacy/private life (see Richardson, 2017; Lake, 2016; Citron, 2022).

References

Abbate, J. (1999). *Inventing the Internet.* Cambridge, MA: MIT Press.

Ackerman, M. S. & Mainwaring, S. D. (2005). Privacy Issues and Human–Computer Interaction. In Cranor L. F. & Garfinkel S., eds., *Security and Usability: Designing Secure Systems that People Can Use.* Sebastopol, CA: O'Reilly, pp. 381–400.

ASIS (1978). *Proceedings of the American Society for Information Science (ASIS): The Information Age in Perspective*, New York, 13–17 November.

Arendt, H. (1949). The Rights Of Man. What Are They?, *Modern Review*, 3, 24–36.

Asimov, I. (1950). *I, Robot.* New York: Gnome Press.

Asimov, I. (1956). The Last Question. *Science Fiction Quarterly*, November, 1–15. Reproduced in Asimov, I. (1986). *Robot Dreams.* New York: Berkley Books, 234–246.

Atten, M. (2013). What Databases Do to Privacy: The Emergence of a Public Issue in 1960s America. *Réseaux*, 178–179(2), 21–53.

Ausloos, J. & Dewitte, P. (2018). Shattering One-Way Mirrors: Data Subject Access Rights in Practice. *International Data Privacy Law*, 8, 4–28.

Ausloos, J., Mahieu, R. & Veale, M. (2019). Getting Data Subject Rights Right. *JIPITEC – Journal of Intellectual Property, Information Technology and E-Commerce Law*, 10, 283–309.

Auxier, B. (2020). Most Americans Support Right to Have some Personal Info Removed from Online Searches. *Pew Research Center*, January 27. https://shorturl.at/UcJGW.

Ayres, I. & Braithwaite, J. (1992). *Responsive Regulation: Transcending the Deregulation Debate.* New York: Oxford University Press.

Bates, E. (2010). *The Evolution of the European Convention on Human Rights from its Inception to the Creation of a Permanent Court of Human Rights.* Oxford: Oxford University Press.

Bell, D. E. & La Padula, L. J. (1976). *Secure Computer System: Unified Exposition and Multics Interpretation, Report ESD-TR-75–306.* Mitre Corporation, Bedford, MA. https://shorturl.at/L7Odg.

Bellman, R. E. (1964). Science, Technology and the Automation Explosion. Paper delivered at the first Annual Conference on the Cybercultural Revolution–Cybernetics and Automation, New York, June 19–21. www.rand.org/content/dam/rand/pubs/papers/2007/P2908.pdf.

Beniger, J. (1986). *The Control Revolution*. Cambridge, MA: Harvard University Press.

Berners-Lee, T. (1999). *Weaving the Web: The Original Design and Ultimate Destiny of the World Wide Web by its Inventor*. New York: Harper Collins.

Big Brother Watch and Others v. the United Kingdom (2021). App nos. 58170/13, 62322/14, 24960/15; Grand Chamber Judgment, ECHR, 25 May 2021; (2022) 74 EHRR 17.

Black, E. (2001). *IBM and the Holocaust*. New York: Crown Publishers.

Bosua, R., Clark, K., Richardson, M. & Webb, J. (2019). Intelligent Warning Systems: 'Technological Nudges' to Enhance User Control of IoT Data Collection, Storage and Use. In Daly, A., Devitt, S. K. & Mann, M., eds., *Good Data*. Amsterdam: Institute of Network Cultures.

Bosua, R., Clifford, D. & Richardson, M. (2023). Contact-Tracing Technologies and the Problem of Trust: Framing a Right of Social Dialogue for an Impact Assessment Process in Pandemic Times. *Law, Technology & Humans*, 5, 193–204.

Brandeis, L. D. (1934). *The Curse of Bigness: Miscellaneous Papers of Louis D. Brandeis*, ed. Fraenkel O. K. & Lewis, C.M. New York: Viking.

Brooker, K. (2018). 'I Was Devastated': Tim Berners-Lee, the Man Who Created the World Wide Web Has Some Regrets. *Vanity Fair Magazine*, 1 July 2018. www.vanityfair.com/news/2018/07/the-man-who-created-the-world-wide-web-has-some-regrets.

Bygrave, L. A. (2002). *Data Protection: Approaching its Rationale, Logic and Limits*. The Hague: Kluwer Law International.

Bygrave, L. A. (2014). *Data Privacy Law: An International Perspective*. Oxford: Oxford University Press.

Bygrave, L. (2020). Article 25 Data Protection by Design and by Default. In Kuner, C., Bygrave, L. A., Docksey, C. & Dreschler, L., eds., *The EU General Data Protection Regulation (GDPR): A Commentary*. Oxford: Oxford University Press, pp. 571–581.

Cain, F. (1990). ASIO and the Australian Labour Movement: An Historical Perspective. *Labour History*, 58, 1–16.

California Consumer Privacy Act (2018). Cal. Civ. Code § 1798.100 et seq.

California Privacy Rights Act (2020). Cal. Civ. Code § 1798.100 et seq.

Celermajer, D. & Lefebvre, A. (2020). Introduction: Bringing the Subject of Human Rights into Focus. In Celermajer, D. & Lefebvre, A., eds., *The Subject of Human Rights*. Stanford, CA: Stanford University Press, pp. 1–26.

Census Act Case, 65 BVerfGE 1 (1983). In Kommers, D. & Miller, R. A. (2012). *The Constitutional Jurisprudence of the Federal Republic of Germany*, 3rd ed. Chapel Hill, NC: Duke University Press, pp. 408–411.

Cerf, V. (1993). *How the Internet Came to Be*. www.netvalley.com/archives/mirrors/cerf-how-inet.html.

Chadd, K. (2020). The History of Cybercrime and Cybersecurity, 1940–2020, *Cybercrime Magazine*, 30 November. https://shorturl.at/QypkQ.

Chander, A., Kaminski, M. E., & McGeveran, W. (2021). Catalyzing Privacy Law, *Minnesota Law Review*, 105, 1733–1802.

Charlesworth, H. (2021). The Travels of Human Rights: The UNESCO Human Rights Exhibition 1950–1953. In Chalmers S. & Pahuja S., eds., *Routledge Handbook of International Law and the Humanities*. Abingdon: Routledge, pp. 173–190.

Cherdantseva, Y. & Hilton, J. (2013). A Reference Model of Information Assurance & Security. In *Proceedings of the 2013 International Conference on Availability, Reliability and Security*, Regensburg, 2–6 September. pp. 546-555.

Citron, D. K. (2022). *The Fight for Privacy: Protecting Dignity, Identity, and Love in the Digital Age*. London: Chatto & Windus.

Clark, D. D. & Wilson, D. R. (1987). A Comparison of Commercial and Military Computer Security Policies. *Proceedings of the IEEE Symposium on Security and Privacy*, Oakland, CA, 27–29 April.

Clifford, D. (2024). *Data Protection Law and Emotion*. Oxford: Oxford University Press.

Clifford, D. & Ausloos, J. (2018). Data Protection and the Role of Fairness, *Yearbook of European Law*, 37, 130–187.

Clifford, D., Goldenfein, J., Jiménez, A. & Richardson, M. (2023). A Right of Social Dialogue on Automated Decision-Making: From Workers' Right to Autonomous Right. *Technology & Regulation*, doi.org/10.26116/techreg.2023.001.

Clifford, D., Richardson, M. & Witzleb, N. (2022). Artificial Intelligence and Sensitive Inferences: New Challenges for Data Protection Law. In Findlay, M., Ford, J., Seah, J. & Thampapillai, D., eds., *Regulatory Insights on Artificial Intelligence: Research for Policy*. Cheltenham: Edward Elgar.

Coase, R. H. (1937). The Nature of the Firm. *Economica*, New Series, 4, 386–405.

Coase, R. H. (1959). The Federal Communications Commission. *Journal of Law & Economics*, 2, 1–40.

Coase, R. H. (1960). The Problem of Social Cost. *Journal of Law & Economics*, 3, 1–44.

Cohen, J. (2019). *Between Truth and Power: The Legal Constructions of Informational Capitalism*. New York: Oxford University Press.

Cohen, J. E. (2021). How (Not) to Write a Privacy Law. *Knight First Amendment Institute*, 23 March. https://knightcolumbia.org/content/how-not-to-write-a-privacy-law.

Cohen-Eliya, M. & Porat, I. (2010). American Balancing and German Proportionality: The Historical Origins. *International Journal of Constitutional Law*, 8, 263–286.

Colomina, B. (1994). *Privacy and Publicity: Modern Architecture as Mass Media*. Cambridge, MA: MIT Press.

Commonwealth of Australia (1988). Privacy Act 1988 (Cth).

Copland v. United Kingdom (2007). ECHR 253.

Council of Europe (1950). *European Convention for the Protection of Human Rights and Fundamental Freedoms, as amended by Protocols Nos. 11 and 14* (ETS 5, 4 November).

Council of Europe (1981). *Convention for the Protection of Individuals with Regard to Automatic Processing of Personal Data* (ETS 108, 28 January).

Council of Europe (2018). Protocol Amending the Convention for the Protection of Individuals with Regard to Automatic Processing of Personal Data (CETS 223, 10 October).

Cowen, Z. (1969). *The Private Man*. The Boyer Lectures 1969. Sydney: Australian Broadcasting Corporation.

Dalla Corte, L. (2020). A Right to a Rule. In Hallinan, D., Leenes, R., Gutwirth, S. & De Hert, P., eds., Data Protection and Privacy: Data Protection and Democracy. Oxford: Hart Publishing, pp. 27–58.

De Búrca, G. (2001). The Drafting of the European Union Charter of Fundamental Rights. *European Law Review*, 26, 126–138.

De Hert, P. (2023). Post-GDPR Lawmaking in the Digital Data Society: Mimesis without Integration. Topological Understandings of Twisted Boundary Setting in EU Data Protection Law. In Curtin, D. & Catanzariti, M., eds., *Data at the Boundaries of European Law*. Oxford: Oxford University Press, pp. 95–132.

De Hert, P. & Gutwirth, S. (2009). Data Protection in the Case Law of Strasbourg and Luxemburg: Constitutionalisation in Action. In Gutwirth, S., Poullet, Y., De Hert, P., Terwangne, C. & Nouwt, S., eds., *Reinventing Data Protection?* Dordrecht: Springer Science, pp. 3–44.

Dembour, M.-B. (2010). What are Human Rights? Four Schools of Thought. *Human Rights Quarterly*, 32, 1–20.

Diggelmann, O. & Cleis, M. N. (2014). How the Right to Privacy Became a Human Right. *Human Rights Law Review*, 14, 441–458.

Digital Rights Ireland (2014): *Digital Rights Ireland Ltd v. Minister for Communications, Marine and Natural Resources and Others and Kärntner Landesregierung and Others*. CJEU, Joined Cases C-293/12 and C-594/12. ECLI:EU:C:2014:238, 8 April.

Doing, S. (2010). Appropriating American Technology in the 1960s: Cold War Politics and the GDR Computer Industry. *IEEE Annals of the History of Computing*, 32(2), 32–45.

Driscoll, K. (2012). From Punched Cards to 'Big Data': A Social History of Database Populism. *Futures of Communication*, 1(1), Article 4.

Editorial Board, Minnesota Law Review (1972). The Fair Credit Reporting Act, *Minnesota Law Review*, 56, 819–841.

European Data Protection Board (2023). 1.2 Billion Euro Fine for Facebook as a Result of EDPB Binding Decision. https://shorturl.at/p5WNd.

European Union (1995). Directive 95/46/EC of the European Parliament and of the Council of 24 October 1995 on the Protection of Individuals with Regard to the Processing of Personal Data and on the Free Movement of Such Data, OJ L 281, pp. 31–50.

European Union (2000, 2007). Charter of Fundamental Rights of the European Union. 2000 OJ C364, 18 December; 2007/C 303/01, 14 December; 2010 OJ (C83) 389, 30 March.

European Union (2007). Treaty of Lisbon Amending the Treaty on European Union and the Treaty Establishing the European Community. Official Journal C 306, 13 December.

European Union (2008). Consolidated Version of the Treaty on European Union and the Treaty of the Functioning of the European Union [2008], OJ C115/13.

European Union (2016). Regulation 2016/679 of the European Parliament and of the Council on the Protection of Natural Persons with Regard to the Processing of Personal Data and on the Free Movement of Such Data, and repealing Directive 95/46/EC (General Data Protection Regulation), 27 April.

European Union (2023). Regulation 2022/2065 of the European Parliament and of the Council on a Single Market for Digital Services and Amending Directive 2000/31/EC (Digital Services Act), 19 October.

European Union (2024a). European Parliament Legislative Resolution on the Proposal for a Regulation of the European Parliament and of the Council on Laying down Harmonised Rules on Artificial Intelligence (Artificial Intelligence Act) and Amending Certain Union Legislative Acts (COM (2021)0206 – C9-0146/2021 – 2021/0106(COD)), 13 March.

European Union (2024b). Directive (EU) 2024/2831 of the European Parliament and of the Council of 23 October 2024 on Improving Working Conditions in Platform Work, OJ L, 2024/2831.

Ewing, K. D., Mahoney, J. & Moretta, A. (2020). *MI5, the Cold War, and the Rule of Law*. Oxford: Oxford University Press.

Federal Republic of Germany (1949). Basic Law for the Federal Republic of Germany, 23 May.

Federal Republic of Germany (1977). Data Protection Act (*Bundesdaten schutzgesetz*:), 27 January.

France (1978). Act 78–17 on Information Technology, Data Files and Individual Liberties (*Loi relative à l'informatique, aux fichiers et aux libertés*), 6 January.

Frohman, L. (2012). 'Only Sheep Let Themselves Be Counted'. Privacy, Political Culture, and the 1983/87 West German Census Boycotts. *Archiv für Sozialgeschichte*, 52, 335–378.

Frohman, L. (2015). Population Registration, Social Planning, and the Discourse on Privacy Protection in West Germany. *Journal of Modern History*, 87, 316–356.

Gajda, A. (2008). What if Samuel D. Warren Hadn't Married a Senator's Daughter? Uncovering the Press Coverage that Led to 'The Right to Privacy'. *Michigan State Law Review*, 2008(1), 35–60.

Gill v. Curtis Publishing Co. (1952). 38 Cal.2d 273, 18 January.

Gill v. Hearst Publishing Co., (1953). 40 Cal.2d 224, 17 February.

Gillies, J. & Cailliau, R. (2000). *How the Web was Born: The Story of the World Wide Web*. New York: Oxford University Press.

González Fuster, G. (2014). *The Emergence of Personal Data Protection as a Fundamental Right of the EU*. Cham: Springer.

González Fuster, G. (2015). Curtailing a Right in Flux: Restrictions of the Right to Personal Data Protection. In Rallo Lombarte, A. & García Mahamut, R., eds., *Hacia un nuevo régimen europeo de protección de datos*. Valencia: Tirant lo Blanch, pp. 513–537.

González Fuster, G. & Gellert, R. (2012). The Fundamental Right of Data Protection in the European Union: In Search of an Uncharted Right. *International Review of Law, Computers & Technology*, 26, 73–82.

Google (2019): *Google LLC v. Commission Nationale de L'informatique et des Libertés (CNIL)*. Case C-507/17, ECLI:EU:C:2019:772, 24 September.

Google Spain (2014): *Google Spain SL & Google Inc. v. Agencia Española de Proteccción de Datos (AEPD) & Mario Costeja González*. Case C-131/12, ECLI:EU:C:2014:317, 13 May.

Gorichanaz, T. & Venkatagiri, S. (2021). The expanding circles of information behavior and human–computer interaction. *Journal of Librarianship and Information Science*, 54(3), 389–403.

Granmar, C. (2021). A Reality Check of the Schrems Saga. *Nordic Journal of European Law*, 4, 48–67.

Griffin, J. (2008). *On Human Rights*. Oxford: Oxford University Press.

Habermas, J. (2010). The Concept of Human Dignity and the Realistic Utopia of Human Rights'. *Metaphilosophy*, 41, 464–480.

Haigh, T. (2001). Inventing Information Systems: The Systems Men and the Computer, 1950–1968. *Business History Review*, 75, 15–61.

Hannah, M. G. (2017). *Dark Territory in the Information Age: Learning from the West German Census Controversies of the 1980s*. London: Routledge.

Hauben, M. (2007). Behind the Net: The Untold History of the ARPANET and Computer Science. In *Netizens: An Anthology*, ch. 7. www.columbia.edu/~rh120.

Hendrix, J. & Lima-Strong, C. (2025). US House Passes 10-Year Moratorium on State AI Laws. *Tech Policy Press*, 23 May. www.techpolicy.press/us-house-passes-10year-moratorium-on-state-ai-laws.

Hesse (1970). Data Protection Act (*Hessische Datenschutzgesetz*), 7 October.

Hilton, A. M. (1966). Foreword. In Hilton, A. M., ed., *The Evolving Society: The Proceedings of the First Annual Conference of the Cybercultural Revolution – Cybernetics and Automation*. New York: Institute for Cybercultural Research. pp. x–xiv.

Hondius, F. W. (1975). *Emerging Data Protection in Europe*. Amsterdam: North Holland Publishing Company.

Hoofnagle, C. J. & Urban, J. M. (2014). Alan Westin's Privacy Homo Economicus. *Wake Forest Law Review*, 49, 261–317.

Hornung, G. & Schnabel, C. (2009). Data Protection in Germany I: The Population Census Decision and the Right to Informational Self-Determination. *Computer Law & Security Review*, 25, 84–88,

James, W. (1907). *Pragmatism, A New Name for some Old Ways of Thinking*. New York: Longmans, Green & Co.

Kaminski, M. E. and Urban, J. M. (2021). The Right to Contest AI. *Columbia Law Review*, 121, 1957–2047.

Kaminski, M. E. (2022). The Case for Data Privacy Rights (or 'Please, a Little Optimism'). *Notre Dame Law Review*, 97, 385–399.

Karas, S. (2002a). Privacy, Identify, Databases. *American University Law Review*, 52, 2(1), 393–445.

Karas, S. (2002b). Enhancing the Privacy Discourse: Consumer Information Gathering as Surveillance. *Journal of Technology Law & Policy*, 7, 29–63.

Kassam, A. (2014). Spain's Everyday Internet Warrior who Cut Free from Google's Tentacles. *The Guardian*, 13 May.

Katz v. United States (1967). 389 U.S. 347, 18 December.

Kempner, R. M. W. (1946). The German National Registration System as Means of Police Control of Population, *Journal of Criminal Law and Criminology*, 36, 362–387.

King, D. B. & Batt, M. A. (1961). Wire Tapping and Electronic Surveillance: A Neglected Constitutional Consideration. *Dickinson Law Review*, 66, 17–38.

Kirby, M. (1983). *Reform the Law: Essays on the Renewal of the Australian Legal System*. Melbourne: Oxford University Press.

Kirby, M. (2011). The History, Achievement and Future of the 1980 OECD Guidelines on Privacy. *International Data Privacy Law*, 6, 1–14.

Kokott, J. & Sobotta, C. (2013). The Distinction between Privacy and Data Protection in the Jurisprudence of the CJEU and the ECtHR. *International Data Privacy Law*, 3, 222–228.

Kommers, D. & Miller, R. A. (2012). *The Constitutional Jurisprudence of the Federal Republic of Germany*, 3rd ed. Chapel Hill, NC: Duke University Press.

Kukutai, T. (2023). Indigenous Data Sovereignty – A New Take on an Old Theme. *Science*, 382, doi.org/10.1126/science.adl4664.

Kukutai, T., Carroll, S. R. & Walter, M. (2020). Indigenous Data Sovereignty. In Mamo, D., ed., *The Indigenous World*, 34th ed. Copenhagen: IWGIA, pp. 654–662.

Kumaraguru, P. & Cranor, L. F. (2005). *Privacy Indexes: A Survey of Westin's Studies*. Institute for Software Research, Carnegie Mellon University, Pittsburgh. http://reports-archive.adm.cs.cmu.edu/anon/isri2005/CMU-ISRI-05-138.pdf.

Lake, J. (2016). *The Face that Launched a Thousand Lawsuits: The American Women who Forged a Right to Privacy*. New Haven: Yale University Press.

Laurer, M. & Seidl, T. (2021). Regulating the European Data-Driven Economy: A Case Study on the General Data Protection Regulation. *Policy & Internet*, 13, 257–277.

Lazcoz, G. & de Hert, P. (2023). Humans in the GDPR and AIA Governance of Automated and Algorithmic Systems: Essential Pre-requisites Against Abdicating Responsibilities. *Computer Law & Security Review*, 50, 1–20.

Lea v. Justice of the Peace, Ltd (1947). *The Times*, 15 March: 2 col. 7.

Lewis, P. H. (1994). Attention Shoppers: Internet is Open. *New York Times*, 12 August.

Licklider, J. C. R. (1960). Man–Computer Symbiosis. *IRE Transactions of Human Factors in Electronics*, HFE-1, 4–11.

Licklider, J. C. R. & Taylor, R. W. (1968). The Computer as a Communication Device. *Science & Technology*, 76, 21–38.

Lindblom, C. E. (1959). The Science of 'Muddling Through'. *Public Administration Review*, 19, 79–88.

Lindqvist (2003): *Bodil Lindqvist*. Case C-101/01, ECLI:EU:C:2003:596.

Luhmann, N. (2004). *Law as a Social System*. Trans. Ziegert, K. A. Oxford: Oxford University Press.

Lynskey, O. (2014). Deconstructing Data Protection in the EU Legal Order. *International and Comparative Law Quarterly*, 63, 569–597.

Lynskey, O. (2015). *The Foundations of EU Data Protection Law*. Oxford: Oxford University Press.

Lynskey, O. (2023). Complete and Effective Data Protection. *Current Legal Problems*, 76, 297–343.

Manne, R. (1987). *The Petrov Affair: Politics and Espionage*. Sydney: Pergamon Press.

Mantelero, A. (2022). *Beyond Data: Human Rights, Ethical and Social Impact Assessment in AI*. The Hague: TMC Asser Press.

Marion Manola v. Stevens & Myers (1890). New York Supreme Court, *New York Times*, June 15, 18, 21.

McCormick, D. W. & Spee, J. C. (2008). IBM and Germany 1922–1941, *Organization Management Journal*, 5, 208–213.

Meta (2023): *Meta Platforms Inc and Others v. Bundeskartellamt*. Case C-252/21, ECLI:EU:C:2023:537, 4 July.

Meta (2022): *Meta Platforms Ireland Limited v. Bundesverband der Verbraucherzentralen und Verbraucherverbände - Verbraucherzentrale Bundesverband eV*. Case C-319/20 ECLI:EU:C:2022:322, 28 April.

Mounier-Kuhn, P.-E. & Pégny, M. (2016). AFCAL and the Emergence of Computer Science in France: 1957–1967. Pursuit of the Universal, June 2016, Paris, France. https://hal.science/hal-01470302v1.

Moyn, S. (2010). *The Last Utopia: Human Rights in History*. Cambridge, MA: Belknap Press of Harvard University Press.

Nader v. General Motors Corporation (1970). 25 N.Y. 2d 560, 8 January.

Nader, R. (1965). Unsafe at Any Speed: The Designed-in Dangers of the American Automobile. New York: Grossman.

Nader, R. (1970). Freedom from Information: The Act and the Agencies. *Harvard Civil Rights-Civil Justice Law Review*, 5, 1–15.

Nelson, R. S. (1997). The Map of Art History. *The Art Bulletin*, 79, 28–40.

Niemietz v. Germany (1992). ECHR 80; (1993) 16 EHRR 97.

Nilsson, E. (2023). Real and Imagined Encounters in the Social History of Surveillance: Soviet Migrants and the Petrov Affair. *Journal of Social History*, 56, 583–606.

Nonet, P. & Selznick, P. ([1978] 2001). *Law & Society in Transition: Toward Responsive Law*, 2nd ed. New Brunswick, NJ: Transaction Publishers.

O'Mara, M. (2018). The End of Privacy Began in the 1960s. *New York Times*, 5 December, www.nytimes.com/2018/12/05/opinion/google-facebook-privacy.html.

O'Regan, G. (2021). *A Brief History of Computing*, 3rd ed. London: Springer.

Olmstead v. United States (1928). 277 U.S. 438, 4 June.

Organisation for Economic Cooperation and Development (OECD) (1980). *Guidelines Governing the Protection of Privacy and Transborder Flow of Personal Data*, 23 September.

Orwell, G. (1949). *Nineteen Eighty-Four*. Oxford: Clarendon Press.

Packard, V. (1964). *The Naked Society: An Exploration of the Mounting Assault on our Privacy by Big Government, Big Business, and Big Education*. New York: D. McKay Co.

Pasquale, F. (2020). *New Laws of Robotics: Defending Human Expertise in the Age of AI*. Cambridge, MA: Belknap Press.

Pasquale, F. (2025). *Data Access and AI Explainability*. New York: Cambridge University Press.

Peers, S. (2011). The Rebirth of the EU's Charter of Fundamental Rights. In Barnard, C. & Odudu, O., eds., *Cambridge Yearbook of European Legal Studies*, 13, pp. 283–310.

Pharmacy Case (1958). 7 BVerfG 377. In Kommers, D. & Miller, R. A. (2012). *The Constitutional Jurisprudence of the Federal Republic of Germany*, 3rd ed. Chapel Hill, NC: Duke University Press, pp. 666–670.

Pilkington, E. (2013). Declassified NSA Files Show Agency Spied on Muhammad Ali and MLK. *The Guardian*, 26 September.

Promusicae (2008): *Productores de Música de España (Promusicae) v. Telefónica de España*. Case C-275/06, ECLI:EU:C:2008:54, 29 January.

Quelle, M. (2018). Enhancing Compliance under the General Data Protection Regulation: The Risky Upshot of the Accountability- and Risk-Based Approach. *European Journal of Risk Regulation*, 9, 502–526.

Radin, M. J. (1989). The Pragmatist and the Feminist. *Southern California Law Review*, 63, 1699–1726.

Riccardi, J. L. (1983). The German Federal Data Protection Act of 1977: Protecting the Right to Privacy? *Boston College International and Comparative Law Review*, 6, 243–271.

Richardson, M. (2015). The Battle for Rights: Getting Data Protection Cases to Court. *Oslow Law Review*, 2, 23–35.

Richardson, M. (2017). *The Right to Privacy: Origins and Influence of a Nineteenth-Century Idea*. Cambridge: Cambridge University Press.

Richardson, M. (2023a). *The Right to Privacy 1914–1948: The Lost Years*. Singapore: Springer.

Richardson, M. (2023b). From Lenah Game Meats to Farm Transparency: Cultures of Privacy and Surveillance in Australia. *Current Legal Issues seminar series*, University of Queensland/Queensland Bar Association, 9 November. https://shorturl.at/PudVV.

Richardson, M., Bosua, R., Clarke, K., Webb. J, Ahmad, A., Maynard, S. (2017). Towards Responsive Regulation of the Internet of Things: Australian Perspectives. *Internet Policy Review*, 6, doi.org/10.14763/2017.1.455.

Risse, M. (2023). *Political Theory of the Digital Age: Where Artificial Intelligence Might Take us*. Cambridge: Cambridge University Press.

Rodotà, S. (2009). Data Protection as a Fundamental Right. In Gutwirth, S. et al., eds., *Reinventing Data Protection?* Dordrecht: Springer Science, pp. 77–82.

Roessler, B. (2017). Privacy as a Human Right. *Proceedings of the Aristotelian Society*, 117, 187–206.

Rundfunk (2003): *Österreichischer Rundfunk and Others*. Case C-139/01, ECLI:EU:C:2003:294.

SABAM v. Netlog (2012): *Sabamelgische Vereniging van Auteurs, Componisten en Uitgevers CVBA (SABAM) v. Netlog NV*. Case C-360/10, ECLI:EU:C:2012:85, 16 February.

Samuel, A. (2017). Meet Alan Emtage, the Black Technologist Who Invented ARCHIE, the First Internet Search Engine. *JSTOR Daily*, February 21. https://daily.jstor.org/alan-emtage-first-internet-search-engine/.

Satamedia (2008): *Tietosuojavaltuutettu v Satakunnan Markkinapörssi Oy and Satamedia Oy*. Case C-73/07, ECLI:EU:C:2008:727.

Scarlet Extended v. SABAM (2011): *Scarlet Extended SA v. Société belge des auteurs, compositeurs et éditeurs SCRL (SABAM)*. Case C-70/10, ECLI:EU:C:2011:771, 11 November.

Schecke & Eifert (2010): *Volker und Markus Schecke GbR and Hartmut Eifert v. Land Hessen*, Joined Cases C-92/09 and C-93/09, ECLI:EU:C:2010:353, 9 November.

Schrems I (2015): *Schrems v. Data Protection Commissioner*. C-362/14, ECLIEU:C:2015:650, 6 October.

Schrems II (2020): *Data Protection Commissioner v. Facebook Ireland Limited, Maximillian Schrems*. C-311/18, ECLI:EU:C:2020:55, 16 July.

Shils, E. & Rheinstein, M. (1954). *Max Weber on Law in Economy and Society*. Trans. Shils, E. & Rheinstein, M. Cambridge, MA: Harvard University Press.

Simitis, S. (2015). Hat der Datenschutz noch eine Chance? Interview by Berndt Frye. Goethe University, Frankfurt. https://rb.gy/mvpl0z.

Solange II (1986): *Re Wünsche Handelsgesellschaft*, BVerfGE 73, 22 October.

Solove, D. J. (2002). Conceptualizing Privacy, *California Law Review*, 90, 1087–1155.

Solove, D. J. (2023). The Limitations of Privacy Rights. *Notre Dame Law Review*, 98, 975–1035.

Solove, D. J. (2024). Murky Consent: An Approach to the Fictions of Consent in Privacy Law. *Boston University Law Review*, 104, 593–639.

Solove, D. J. (2025). *On Privacy and Technology*. New York: Oxford University Press.

Spafford, E. (1988). *The Internet Worm Program: An Analysis*. Purdue Technical Report CSD-TR-823. Purdue University, West Lafayette, IN. https://spaf.cerias.purdue.edu/tech-reps/823.pdf.

Stadler, G. & Herzog, T. (1982). *Data Protection: International Trends and the Austrian Example*. IIASA Collaborative Paper. Laxenburg: International Institute for Applied Systems Analysis. https://core.ac.uk/download/pdf/33893567.pdf.

Sweden (1973). Data Act (*Datalagen*), 1 July.

Thomas, J., Burgess, J., Angus, D. & Lawrence, A. (2022). Building an Australian Social Data Observatory. *Innovation Papers*, June 2022, 31–32. https://internetobservatory.org.au/post/blog-post-three-tbsem.

Turing, A. M. (1950). Computing Machinery and Intelligence, *Mind*, 59, 433–460.

Tzanou, M. (2013). Data Protection as a Fundamental Right Next to Privacy? 'Reconstructing' a Not so New Right. *International Data Privacy Law*, 3, 88–99.

UN General Assembly (1948). Universal Declaration of Human Rights, A/RES/217(III), 10 December.

UN General Assembly (1966). International Covenant on Civil and Political Rights, 16 December.

UN Human Rights Committee (1988). CCPR General Comment No. 16: Article 17 (Right to Privacy), The Right to Respect of Privacy, Family, Home and Correspondence, and Protection of Honour and Reputation, 8 April.

United States Congress (1974). The Privacy Act of 1974, Public Law 93–579, 31 December.

United States House of Representatives Special Subcommittee (1965). *Invasion of Privacy*, 2, 3, 4, and 23 June and 23 September.

United States House of Representatives Special Subcommittee (1966). *The Computer and Invasion of Privacy*, 26–28 July.

US Department of Health, Education & Welfare (1973). *Records, Computers and the Rights of Citizens*. Report of the Secretary's Advisory Committee on

Automated Personal Data Systems. DHEW Publication NO. (OS), 73–94. www.justice.gov/opcl/docs/rec-com-rights.pdf.

Van Der Sloot, B. (2017). Legal Fundamentalism: Is Data Protection Really a Fundamental Right? In Leenes, R., van Brakel, R., Gutwirth, S. & De Hert, P., eds., *Data Protection and Privacy: (In)visibilities and Infrastructures.* Cham: Springer, pp. 3–30.

Victoria Park Racing & Recreation Grounds Co Ltd v. Taylor (1937). 58 CLR 479, 26 August.

Von Jhering, R. (1879). *The Struggle for Law (Der Kampf um's Recht*, 5th ed., 1877). Trans. Lalor, J. J. Chicago: Callaghan & Co.

Waldman, A. E. (2022). Privacy's Rights Trap, *Northwestern University Law Review*, 117, 88–106.

Ware, W. H. (1979). *Security Controls for Computer Systems: Report of Defence Science Board Task Force on Computer Security.* U.S. Department of Defense (DoD), R-609–1. Santa Monica: Rand Corporation.

Ware, W. H. (1980). Privacy and Information Technology: The Years Ahead. In Hoffman, L. J., ed., *Computers and Privacy in the Next Decade.* New York: Academic Press, pp. 9–22.

Warren, S. D. & Brandeis, L. D. (1890). The Right to Privacy. *Harvard Law Review*, 4, 193–220.

Weber, M. (1922). *Economy and Society [Soziologische Kategorienlehre].* Ed. and trans. Tribe, K. Cambridge, MA: Harvard University Press, 2019.

Westin, A. F. (1967). *Privacy and Freedom.* New York: Atheneum.

Westin, A. F. & Baker M.A. (1972). *Databanks in a Free Society: Computers, Record-Keeping, and Privacy.* Report by Project on Computer Databanks (National Academy of Sciences). New York: Quadrangle Books.

Westin, A. F. & Baker M. A. (1973). Databanks in a Free Society. *ACM SIGCAS Computers and Society*, 4I, 25–29.

Whitman M. E. & Mattord, H. E. (2021). *Management of Information Security*, 6th ed. Boston, MA: Cengage.

Wiener, N. (1948). *Cybernetics: Or Control and Communication in the Animal and the Machine.* Cambridge, MA: MIT Press.

Wiener, N. (1950). *The Human Uses of Human Beings: Cybernetics and Society.* Boston: Houghton Mifflin Co.

Yeung, K. & Bygrave, L. A. (2021). Demystifying the Modernized European Data Protection Regime: Cross-Disciplinary Insights from Legal and Regulatory Governance Scholarship. *Regulation & Governance*, 16, 137–155.

Zuboff, S. (2019). *The Age of Surveillance Capitalism: The Fight for a Human Future at the New Frontier of Power.* New York: PublicAffairs.

Acknowledgements

This Element has benefited immeasurably from the information and ideas contributed by our friends, colleagues, and students over the years. But we particularly want to acknowledge the valuable critical advice and support of our editors, Claes Granmar and Jeannie Paterson, and the insightful comments we received from Frank Pasquale and Julian Thomas, who generously read earlier drafts. We also thank Daniel Woolf for inspiring us to set up the Element series in which this Element features, and Kristen Rundle for helpful practical advice about beginning a new Element project and seeing it through to fruition. Finally, special thanks are owed to Cambridge University Press and especially Matthew Gallaway, Adam Hooper, and Jaydn Fauconier-Herry for excellent professional care and guidance.

Cambridge Elements

Data Rights and Wrongs

Megan Richardson
University of Melbourne

Megan Richardson is Honorary Professor at the Melbourne Law School, the University of Melbourne. Her research covers privacy and data rights, law reform and legal theory. Her books include *The Right to Privacy: Origins and Influence of a Nineteenth-Century Idea* (2017); *Research Handbook on Intellectual Property in Media and Entertainment Law* (ed with Sam Ricketson, 2017); *Advanced Introduction to Privacy Law* (2020); and *The Right to Privacy 1914–1948: The Lost Years* (2023).

Rachelle Bosua
Deakin University

Rachelle Bosua is Senior Lecturer at Deakin University and Honorary Senior Fellow in the School of Computing and Information Systems at the University of Melbourne. She was previously an assistant professor at the Open University Netherlands. Her research considers the role and use of data in digital contexts, including data privacy and ethics, design and adoption of digital artefacts in remote and platform-based work, knowledge leakage and digital innovation. She is a co-author of *Knowledge Management in Organizations: A Critical Introduction* (with Donald Hislop and Remko Helms, 4th ed, 2018).

Damian Clifford
Australian National University

Damian Clifford is Senior Lecturer in Law at the Australian National University and an associate researcher at the Information Law and Policy Centre at the Institute of Advanced Legal Studies (University of London). Previously an FWO aspirant fellow at KU Leuven's Centre for IT and IP Law (CiTiP), his research focuses on privacy, data protection and technology regulation, and he has published across these fields. His recent books are *Data Rights and Private Law* (ed. with Jeannie Marie Paterson and Kwan Ho Lau, 2023) and *Data Protection Law and Emotions* (2024).

Jake Goldenfein
University of Melbourne

Jake Goldenfein is Senior Lecturer at the Melbourne Law School, the University of Melbourne. Previously a researcher at Cornell Tech, Cornell University, and New York Law School, his work spans media and communications history and theory, communications policy, privacy and media law. Current areas of focus are mechanism design, algorithmic transparency, and decision-making accountability. His book *Monitoring Laws: Profiling and Identity in the World State* was published in 2020.

Jeannie Marie Paterson
University of Melbourne

Jeannie Marie Paterson is Director of the Centre for AI and Digital Ethics at the University of Melbourne and Professor of Law at the Melbourne Law School. Her research focuses on themes of support for vulnerable consumers; the regulation of new technologies in consumer and financial markets; and regulatory design for protecting consumer rights and promoting safe, fair and accountable technologies. Her recent books include *Misleading Silence* (ed. with Elise Bant, 2020) and *Data Rights and Private Law* (ed. with Damian Clifford and Kwan Ho Lau, 2023).

Julian Thomas
RMIT University

Julian Thomas is Director of the ARC Centre of Excellence for Automated Decision-Making and Society, and Distinguished Professor in the School of Media and Communication at RMIT University, in Melbourne. He has written widely about digital inclusion, automation and other topics relating to the pasts and futures of new communications and computing technologies. His books include *The Informal Media Economy* (2015), *Internet on the Outstation: The Digital Divide and Remote Aboriginal Communities* (2016) and *Wi-Fi* (with Ellie Rennie and Rowan Wilken, 2021).

Editorial Board

Mark Andrejevic, *Professor, Communications & Media Studies, Monash Data Futures Institute*

Sara Bannerman, *Professor, McMaster University, and Canada Research Chair in Communication Policy & Governance*

Claes Granmar, *Associate Professor, Faculty of Law, Stockholm University*

Sonia Katyal, *Associate Dean of Faculty Development & Research, Co-Director of Berkeley Center for Law & Technology, Roger J Traynor Distinguished Professor of Law, UC Berkeley*

Andrew Kenyon, *Professor of Law, Melbourne Law School, University of Melbourne*

Orla Lynskey, *Professor of Law and Technology, University College London*

Frank Pasquale, *Professor of Law, Cornell Tech and Cornell Law School, New York*

Trisha Ray, *Associate Director and Resident Fellow, GeoTech Center, Atlantic Council*

Peggy Valcke, *Professor of Law & Technology and Vice-Dean of Research, Faculty of Law & Criminology, KU Leuven*

Normann Witzleb, *Associate Professor of Law, Chinese University of Hong Kong*

About the Series

This Cambridge Elements series provides a home for fresh arguments about data rights and wrongs along with legal, ethical and other responses. We encourage new ways of thinking about data as enmeshed within social, institutional and technical relations.

Cambridge Elements

Data Rights and Wrongs

Elements in the Series

Data Rights in Transition
Rachelle Bosua, Damian Clifford, Jing Qian and Megan Richardson

A full series listing is available at: www.cambridge.org/EDRW

For EU product safety concerns, contact us at Calle de José Abascal, 56–1°,
28003 Madrid, Spain or eugpsr@cambridge.org.

www.ingramcontent.com/pod-product-compliance
Lightning Source LLC
LaVergne TN
LVHW011857060526
838200LV00054B/4392